MODELING
MILITARY FIGURES

Painting uniforms, skin tones, and weapons with realistic accuracy

by Joe Hudson

Kalmbach
Media

On the Cover: Clockwise from left, Alpine U.S. Infantry NSO, Chapter 7; Tarter Miniatures Field Marshal Montgomery, Chapter 6; and Scale 75 War Front Private First Class, Chapter 7.

Kalmbach Media
21027 Crossroads Circle
Waukesha, Wisconsin 53186
www.KalmbachHobbyStore.com

All photos were taken by the author, unless otherwise noted.

Please follow appropriate health and safety measures when working with materials and equipment. Some general guidelines are presented in this book, but always read and follow the manufacturers' instructions.

Published in 2023
27 26 25 24 23   1 2 3 4 5

Manufactured in China

ISBN: 978-1-62700-939-3
EISBN: 978-1-62700-940-9

Photos: Joe Hudson
Editor: Mark Savage
Book Design: Lisa Bergman and Lisa Schroeder

Library of Congress Control Number: 2022945621

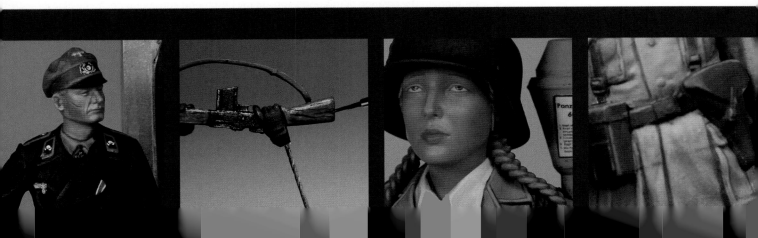

I have so many people to acknowledge and thank, but before I do, I want to thank my Lord and Savior, Jesus Christ, and God, my Heavenly Father, for all the wonderful blessings, opportunities and abilities given me.

First, I would like to thank my wonderful editors, Eric White and Mark Savage, for their help and support throughout my journey of writing this book. I would also like to acknowledge a few whose support I am especially grateful for.

To my good friend Rick Hill, with whom I spent many hours discussing, building, and painting models while we worked together at Cape Canaveral Air Force Station. Also, my friend Big Al Presley, who was always there to take my phone calls when I needed a break from painting. I also wish to thank by friend Bill Chilstrom for always answering my endless questions. Special thanks to Kevin Thompson for taking some great photos of the work in this book, and Jerry Dean and Chad Weyenberg for their help with a few

important project details.

Thanks also to Tony Jaros, Marc Fraley, Omar Baez, Kenny Conklin, and Oggie Gonzalez, who provided invaluable feedback along this journey.

I have been personally blessed to get to know, admire, and now call friends so many wonderful artists and sculptors in this hobby over the past few decades. I have learned so much from so many that's it's impossible to name everyone so please forgive me for any omissions.

I thank the late Bob Letterman for sharing his wisdom and providing me with hours of amazement with his work along with his lovely wife, Susan, who first introduced me to figure shows. I would also like to acknowledge the late Shep Paine, who was an inspiration and whose book *How to Build Dioramas* has kept me occupied for years.

Many thanks also to Bill Horan, Doug Cohen, Mike Stelzel, Ron Souza, Rod Curtis, Phil Kessling, Brian Howard, and Charlie Pritchett for answering my endless questions. I would also like to thank my friend Brett Avants for introducing me to my wonderful wife!

A big thank you to my parents for supporting me in this hobby since I was a kid. You put up with me when I locked myself in my room listening to loud music and building monster models. A thank you also to my brothers and sisters for their endless support. Love you all!

Finally, to my wife, Carissima, who listened, encouraged, and critiqued my work throughout the creation of this book. You are my best friend and soulmate. To my oldest son, Ethan, who always enjoyed traveling to figure shows with his "Pop", thanks for all the memories and keeping me company on the trips. And to my youngest son, Brody, who always finds a way to make me smile. I am forever thankful for your loving support.

And one more thank you, to you, the readers. I hope you find this book both helpful and enjoyable.

Joe Hudson

I met Joe Hudson about 30 years ago. He was one of the original Master's Group members of VLS Corp. Joe is an unassuming guy who is a joy to hang out with. He started modeling as most of us did, building planes, armor, and so on.

Around 1989, he got into figure painting after having been in a motorcycle accident. He attended many Mastercon conventions in St. Louis, Mo., and my wife, Susan, told him about the Atlanta figure show.

Joe had begun painting Verlinden 120mm figures and attended the Atlanta show, where he met Bob Knee, a well-known American figure painter who, unfortunately, is no longer with us. Bob went to visit Joe in Florida and gave him a weekend painting lesson. That motivated Joe on the path to his figure-painting career.

Joe later moved to the St. Louis area where I lived. He learned his skills quickly and even began sculpting his own figures. As his skills grew, he began sculpting for Verlinden. He sculpted for me at VLS in the "Streets of Laredo" Wild West range as well as the VLS Custom Dioramics line. Joe also has created box art for many companies, including Verlinden, my lines, Thunderbird Miniatures, Michael Roberts Ltd., and others.

Joe has won gold medals at Shep Paine's Chicago Show in both the Painters and Open division, doing the same at the MFCA (Miniature Figure Collectors of America), the Atlanta show, and the National Capital Model Society. He was awarded the title of Grandmaster at the Tulsa figure show and went on to garner awards at the prestigious World Model Expo International conventions in Canada, Scotland, Boston, and Chicago.

Joe has also won numerous "Best of" categories at those shows including "Best of the West," "Best Napoleonic," "Scotland Forever," as well as "People's Choice." Further, Joe has won several Best of Shows at Missouri and Florida model figure conventions. As a Master's member of VLS, he also has won many gold medals at Mastercon!

Joe has been happily married to his lovely wife, Carissima, for 22 years and is the proud father of two sons, Ethan, a college junior on a football scholarship, and Brody, a college sophomore on an academic scholarship and who also is on the track and cross-country teams. The family has two awesome dogs, Gracie and Roman.

This is Joe's first book. I am sure you will enjoy it and that there will be more to come. I am proud to call Joe my friend!

Bob Letterman

I would like to dedicate this book to our old man Watson. Rest In Peace, Watty!

Bob Letterman photo

Editor's note: Sadly, just a few months before this book was sent to the printer, Bob Letterman passed away. We extend our sympathies to his family and friends.

PAINTING WITH ACRYLICS

Getting started painting with acrylics requires learning a few things and figuring out a few more. I will discuss these and explain some of the things that I have learned to use with some success.

There are pros and cons to using acrylics. Some say they dry too quickly, while others love that they dry quickly! I will show the benefits of both sides.

There are many manufacturers of acrylic paints. The great thing is that most paint brands will mix well with each other.

Some brands are slightly different from each other, but what you use will come down to your own personal preference about which brand you like best.

As you go through this book you will see that I use many brands of acrylics, and I have learned (as you will) which ones work best for me in certain applications. For example, Vallejo Flat Black may appear less flat than, say, Scale 75 Flat Black.

Water: Painting with acrylics will require using water to thin your paint. You can use regular tap water or distilled water. I use distilled water because years ago I was using a certain manufacturer's brand and it reacted with the chemicals in my tap water, causing my figure to become chalky. After that I switched to distilled water and have not had any problems in 20 years.

Another factor to consider when painting with acrylics is that they all must be thoroughly mixed before using them. It is important to shake them well to make sure they are fully mixed before using.

For instance, if you squeeze out the paint and see a white color, that is the carrier, and you have not properly mixed the paint. You'll need to shake it a bit longer.

Painting with acrylics can, and will, be both rewarding and sometimes frustrating!

I can say this from experience. If you are struggling with one thing the next object or project may be the most rewarding, so do not give up!

Before starting to paint, here are a few things that you should know so that your painting experience will go as smoothly as possible.

1: BASE COATS

The base coat will be your initial coverage of a particular color. This should cover the whole area, but not be so thick that it obscures the details of the area you are painting.

Base coats are applied using two or three thin layers of paint. Since you're using acrylics, you can use a hair dryer between applying the layers to help speed the process.

2: HIGHLIGHTS

The highlight is the application of a lighter shade of paint to simulate where the light source would hit the area from above.

The application of this process is like base coating, but the paint will need to be thinner, like a glaze, to avoid leaving brush strokes on that area.

Applying highlights may take anywhere from 3 to 7 layers, depending on the color or intensity you are trying to achieve.

3: SHADOWS

Shadows are remarkably similar in applying highlights, except that in this process we are trying to simulate where the light source does not hit an area, creating a shadow.

Shadows are also applied using several layers of thin paint in glazes, as well.

4: GLAZES

A glaze is an application of very thin paint over another layer of paint that you are applying to an area to achieve a desired effect such as a highlight or shadow.

A typical glaze ratio is approximately 1 drop of paint to 2 drops of water.

5: WASHES

A wash is a heavily diluted mixture of paint and water. A wash is mainly used to flow into creases, crevices, and grooves. A wash helps bring out definition of the area that you are working on.

A typical wash ratio is approximately 1 drop of paint to 3 or 4 drops of water.

6: DRY-BRUSHING

Dry-brushing has been used quite often in modeling and even figure painting. Dry-brushing is used to bring out the raised areas or details on a certain area. I use dry-brushing at a minimum when painting a figure, but I will sometimes use this method to help show me where to apply highlights and shadows.

Dry-brushing is exactly what it says. It is the process of taking a dry brush and dipping it into paint, not using any water, then wiping the excess paint off the brush with a paper towel or rag before lightly going over the areas to bring out the raised surface details with the minimal paint left on the brush.

7: OUTLINING

Outlining is used to delineate one area from another. This is used to show seams, separate one item from another, etc. This line is usually darker and next to a lighter one.

You can create this outline by using one dark line or by building it up with thinner light ones. It is important to keep these lines as clean and crisp as possible. This is where it is vital to have a brush with a sharp point that can also hold enough paint to make the lines full length in the area where you are working.

Finally, before you begin painting, it's important to know how to unload your brush. Here's how I do it.

Unloading a brush: Naturally you start by first dipping the brush into the paint and loading it up just as you are about to paint a figure or portion of one. Next, take the brush from the paint, and wipe it with a rolling motion on a paper towel or soft cloth. This gets the excess paint out of the brush and makes sure that the tip has been rolled to a point. Doing this will help prevent applying a runny layer of paint in the area you are working on.

I prefer to use blue paper towels that are usually found in car repair shops, as these do not usually have extra fibers or lint that could contaminate your paint.

TOOLS

Essential gear to get you going

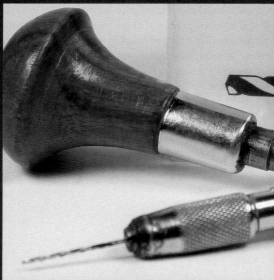

There are several tools that you will need to begin any project, whether building a model or a figure. Then there are other tools that you do not necessarily have to own, but will make the process a bit easier. I will explain the ones that I have and use on almost all projects.

1.1 Sandpapers, Files, Putties, Glues and other Essentials

SANDPAPERS

There are many different choices you can use for sandpapers. I have used a wide variety, but my favorite is the foam sanding pad that I buy from my local paint store. They have a variety of sandpaper, foam sanding pads and Scotch Brites.

I prefer the foam pads because they are flexible and can fit into nearly any area, conforming to the different parts and shapes that need sanding.

FILES

This is another basic tool you'll need for initial cleanup of model parts. I picked up this small set many years ago at a figure competition, but you can find similar files on the internet. These are good for getting into places that the sandpaper/sponge cannot reach and also come in handy when you are trying to remove a mold line or seam from a fold.

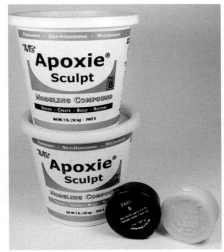

PUTTIES

Putties, and there are many, help fill a gap where two parts meet and when there is a seam that is noticeable once you glue parts together. For the most part these putties are really good for filling smaller seams, but there are times where you will need to fill a bigger seam or make corrections to a part that will need some resculpting. This is where you will need something like a two-part epoxy sculpting compound.

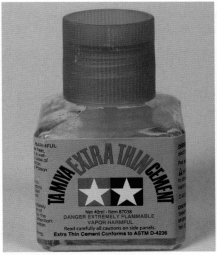

GLUES

You are going to need some type of glue to assemble your kit/figure, and the type depends on the material you are working with – plastic, vinyl, resin, or metal.

If you are building a plastic model, you will need glue designed for that material. I prefer Tamiya liquid glue, the bottle with the green top, for my work. This solvent works well to melt the plastics together and form a strong bond.

When building a resin figure or attaching vinyl, you will need something other than modeling glues. Cyanoacrylate adhesive (CA), also known as "super glue," is best. I use the medium version from my hobby shop as it gives me a little bit of time (not much) before setting. It also is not too thin or runny, nor too thick.

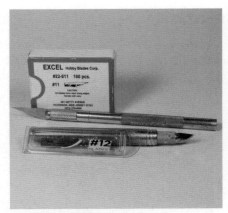

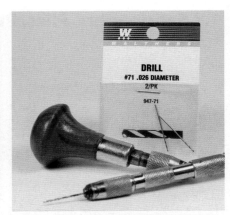

HOBBY KNIVES

The essential tool for modelers is a hobby knife for removing extraneous plastic from model or figure parts. There are many choices of knives and blades, and some modelers even use scalpels. I use a standard X-Acto knife with two different blades: a No. 11 pointed and No. 12 curved. I prefer the curved blade for getting into folds or angles where a straight blade just cannot reach without damaging a part.

CUTTERS

To cleanly cut parts from a sprue or casting block, you'll want a good set of cutters. If you take care of them, good cutters will last for years.

DRILL BITS AND HAND DRILLS

When altering figures you'll need small drill bits of varying size to add pins to a figure's feet or even pin other parts to a figure. For example, you may want to drill a head before pinning it so you can paint it separately, then re-attach the head to the figure after finishing other areas.

NOT NECESSARY, BUT HELPFUL TOOLS

There are five other items that are not absolutely necessary but do come in handy and will make your life easier. Some are easily found and inexpensive, such as rounded toothpicks and a fiberglass pen. But you also may wish to keep an old electric toothbrush and a hair dryer handy. Finally, I recommend a pair of head-mounted magnifiers; one brand is Optivisor. Here's how you'll use these items.

A fiberglass pen helps get into very tight areas and remove unwanted material. The down side to a fiberglass pen is that broken pieces of the fiberglass can stick in your fingers or other skin. So be careful. I often use rubber gloves when handling one.

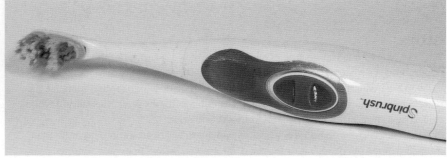

Toothpicks are good for applying super glue or modeling putty, or even helping to open the clog in a bottle of paint. You can also attach parts temporarily to toothpicks while you paint them.

An old electric toothbrush is handy for helping remove residue when you're finished sanding a part. I have also used a toothbrush to clean a part by dipping the bristles in rubbing alcohol and running it along the part.

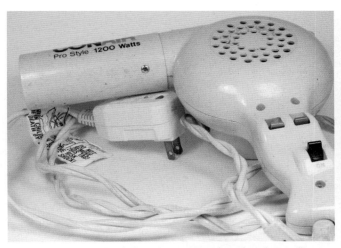

Though it's not essential, if you keep a hair dryer handy, you'll find yourself using it quite often. I use it to speed up drying times between paint layers. This helps me complete projects more quickly than I would have by just waiting for the paint to dry on its own.

A magnifier is a blessing when working on small details, especially when painting tiny items such as belt buckles or buttons. Magnifiers come with different powers of magnification. A good starting point is a No. 5 lens, but I generally use a No. 10 lens.

1.2 Palettes (Wet and Porcelain)

There are several types of palettes available for painting with acrylics. The two I use most are a wet palette and a porcelain one.

The wet palette consists of a tray, cover, sponge, and hydration paper. Here's how it works.

You will have a wet sponge that has a piece of hydration paper over it where you will add your paints and then mix them on the paper. The benefit is that you can stop with a project, put the cover on, and come back later to continue working, because your paints are still use-able, having not dried up.

My porcelain palette features 24 small wells. I have used this method for a long time, much longer than the wet palette. Its benefit is that you can make different mixes in the wells. The downside is that the mixes eventually dry out, meaning you'll have to mix the colors again. However, this is not much of a problem if you keep your mixes simple.

While I have used both, I now prefer the wet palette.

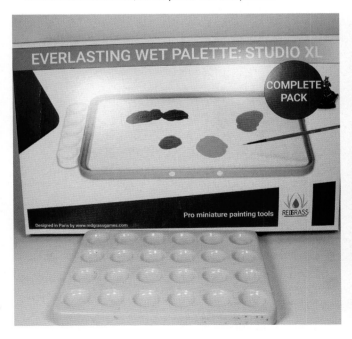

1.3 Paints and Thinners

PAINTS

There are many brands and types of acrylic paints. Each is only as good as the person using them. I have seen masterpieces painted with cheap craft paints as well as masterpieces done using hobby acrylics. Don't get caught up in buying everything. First see which type works best for you and then learn to master it.

I have used craft paints, but find them too hard for me to work with, so I tend to use only hobby paints. Each brand has its own qualities and colors, but you can mix and match brands without worrying about having bad reactions.

There are varying box sets of paints too. Buying these is a good way to collect a variety of colors. These sets, which can benefit both beginners and experienced painters, are designed to help a painter avoid needing to mix a lot of paints to achieve a specific color. You will find sets that have basic flesh colors, certain uniform colors, or just a variation on one color.

With experience you also will find that some of the box sets may have a color that you can use for something totally different. For example, the dark red shadow from the flesh set may also serve as a great base color for a British paratrooper's beret.

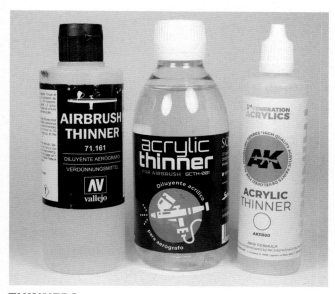

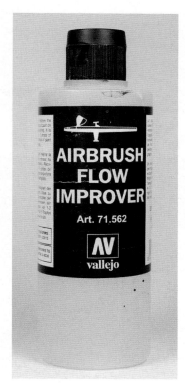

FLOW MEDIUM

A flow medium is another item that can help both beginners and experienced painters. A medium is a good extender, helping to keep the paint from drying too quickly. It also helps when you are painting a longer/larger area by preventing brush strokes and can help keep the point on your brush tight when painting small details.

THINNERS

Most companies offer their own acrylic thinner. These are designed to be used with an airbrush, but they also can be used with brush painting. Fortunately, if you are not using them with an airbrush, it's not necessary to use only the paint brand's thinner. For example, if you have an AK Interactive color that you like, you can use Scale 75 thinner.

1.4 Primers

When you are cleaning up a figure or want to see if a figure is ready to paint, you will need to prime it. Primer comes in several colors. I prefer light gray because I feel it is easier to see any imperfections that I may have missed. Many painters prefer black primer, but either way, once your figure is clean and ready, a primer coat will provide a consistent base for you to begin painting details.

There are different ways to apply a primer coat. You can spray it from the can, dispense it so it can be brushed on, or decant it for use in an airbrush. My preference is to spray Tamiya Sky Gray (XF-19) through my airbrush.

1.5 Paint-brushes

The paintbrush is your most important tool when it comes to painting figures. Like everything else there are many types, brands, and sizes to choose from, ranging from cheap to extremely expensive. Bristles can be either nylon or natural materials.

There are pros and cons to each. I prefer non-nylon brushes for most of my figure painting work but occasionally use nylons for ground work or metals. The one essential for detail work (painting a face or eyes) is a brush that

maintains a good point and that can hold the correct amount of paint needed for the application.

My brushes of choice are from ZEM and RedgrassGames. They are natural hair and hold their point extremely well, plus they are quite durable. My preferred sizes are No. 1, No. 2, and No. 2/0.

Another good choice are natural hair brushes from The Brushman. One set, SP Extra Short Detail brushes, come in handy.

I also absolutely love Tamiya's Modeling Brush Pro II (No. 87172). This is a natural brush but extremely small and holds an amazing point.

Again, I do not use nylon brushes to paint figures. I have not found a nylon brush that can properly hold a point, the primary concern for figure painting. There may be some out there, but I prefer natural materials.

ASSEMBLING FIGURES

How to prepare and put together plastic, resin, and metal kits

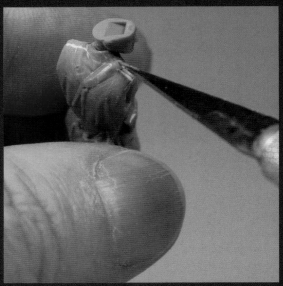

Figures are available in plastic, resin, and even white metal. Each has its pros and cons.

For 1/35 scale and smaller figures the most common material will either be injection-molded plastic or resin. In this chapter I will discuss both materials while also showing you the tools that I use, how to remove the different parts from their respective carriers, and cleanup of the parts. Then we'll move on to assembly using model glue and super glue, filling the gaps and seams using putties, and a few other tips to add details to your figures to make them a little more appealing or interesting.

When building either plastic or resin figures I use a good pair of cutters, a hobby knife with a No. 11 blade, a minibrush with fiberglass bristles, fine foam sanding pads, Scotch-Brite (red) sanding pad, and an old electric toothbrush.

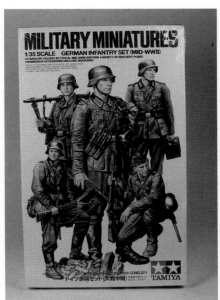

Here I'll use the figures from my "Propaganda" diorama (more in Chapter 8) as examples of how to assemble plastic and resin figures. For this diorama I used Tamiya's German Infantry Mid-WWII set (No. 35371) as plastic figure examples and Bravo 6 Herr Officer (B6-35133) as the resin figure.

2.1 Assembling Plastic Figures

Upon opening the box, you'll find a few bags containing several sprues with all the parts. At close inspection, the parts are well-molded and crisply executed.

Decide which figure you want to build first. Next, I use my sprue cutters to remove parts from the sprues. I prefer the nippers from Redgrass Games because they have a flat surface on one side and are very sharp. Get close to the part and nip it off.

Once the parts have been removed, you will be left with a little nub on your figure. The size of this will vary depending on how close you were able to get when removing the part from the sprue.

To remove the nub, use a hobby knife to carefully and slowly remove the excess plastic.

Once these nubs are removed, I remove the seam lines on each part. I use the back side of my hobby knife blade in a scraping fashion.

Next, take a small piece of sanding foam to smooth and polish the previously worked areas.

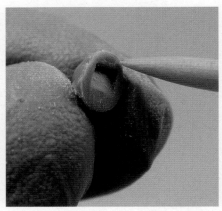

Here you can see the finished result on the top of the figure's head after removing the excess plastic.

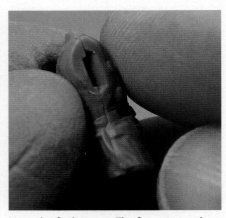

Next, dry-fit the parts. The first purpose here is to see if the parts line up. The second is to see if any filler will be needed once the parts are glued together.

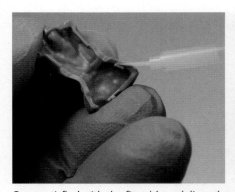

Once satisfied with the fit, add modeling glue to the parts. I use Tamiya Extra Thin glue.

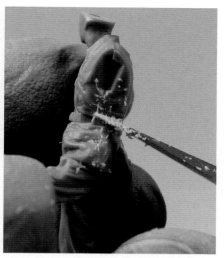

Once I've assembled a section of the figure, there is a slight gap where the parts were glued together. Sometimes these gaps are larger and require putty, but often, like here, small gaps are filled in with the melting of the plastic by the glue ...

... then I use a hobby knife and repeat the process as before in removing the seam lines.

You can see that a lot of the excess has been removed with this process.

I then use the sanding foam to sand the previously worked areas. I try to get this area as smooth as possible without removing or destroying surrounding details.

Once the sanding is completed, I use a section of the Scotch-Brite and polish the previously sanded areas, again being careful of the surrounding details.

Here is the result of using the knife, sanding foam, and Scotch-Brite. I am left with a nice, smooth area.

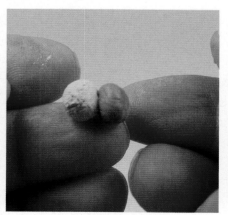
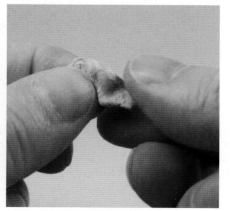

Next, I fill in any minor seams using Deluxe Perfect Plastic Putty before beginning to work on each figure, correcting imperfections, and enhancing some of their parts. For any larger seams or imperfections, I will use Aves Apoxie Sculpt. This is a two-part putty where you mix equal parts so that it will cure and harden. Curing time is usually about one hour. Take two small equal amounts of the Part A and Part B putties and mix them using a twisting motion until the mix is a uniform color, in this case a grayish white.

After mixing the putty, place a small amount on the section of the shoulders where the harness straps are missing.

Next, take a soft, damp brush and gently press it down onto the areas before smoothing it.

Once the putty has been smoothed and is relatively flat, I take a sharp hobby knife blade and remove the excess on each side. I follow the contours of the strap that were already there in plastic.

After correcting the shoulder harnesses on the figures, I noticed one of the soldiers looked rather thin. To correct this I again used the Aves and filled in the folds following the same procedure using the moist brush to smooth the putty to fill out his pant legs. You can see that I have already filled in the left leg, but there is a void in the right leg fold,. I will apply more putty to thicken it.

2.2 Assembling Resin Figures

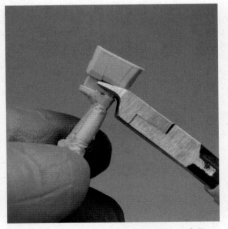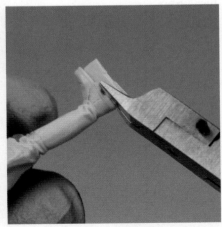

The German Herr Officer kit consists of 4 resin parts: the body, head, left arm and holster, mounted on carrier blocks, typical of resin.

The carrier blocks need to be removed. For this I again use sprue cutters, being careful to cut the parts off close to the block.

Now that the big block has been removed, I get as close as I can to remove the excess resin from the bottom of the boots.

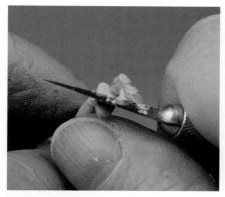
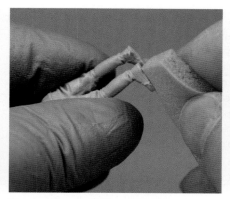
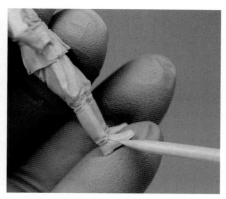

Next I clean up the boot bottoms with a hobby knife. Carefully remove as much as you can using the front and back of the blade without damaging the part.

Once all the remaining carriers have been removed, I sand the part to a clean finish using foam sanding pads.

Resin figures sometimes have a seam or casting line that will need to be removed. Most times these are very faint, but if not correctly cast, the lines may be more prominent.

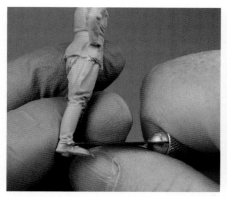
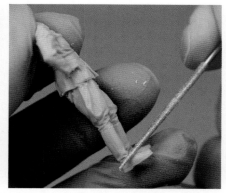

To remove these lines, I use both my hobby knife and miniature files. When using files, be careful not to sand too hard or you could remove too much material.

Next, dry-fit the parts before gluing. This is a more important step with resin than with plastic, because with resin you must attach the parts using super glue, and you won't have much time to make corrections.

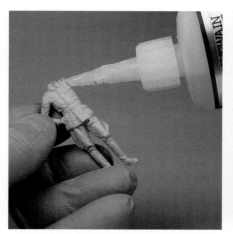

Once deciding the fit is good, use super glue to attach the parts, then add a drop of CA accelerant such as Zip Kicker to accelerate curing. Here's a tip I've learned over the years in applying Zip Kicker. Just open the bottle, remove the top, which has a siphon tube in it, then apply the kicker in spots sparingly. By doing this you do not waste as much as if you used the usual spraying technique.

2.3 Filling Seams

With either a plastic or resin figure, once assembly is complete there usually will be a seam or gap between parts. This does not happen all the time, but when it does, there are several ways to correct the problem.

Usually with a plastic figure I use one of the tube-type filler putties. For resin figures I use Aves epoxy putty. This is a general rule of thumb, but I sometimes use both kinds of putties on both plastic and resin figures.

An example of a seam that needs to be corrected here is where the holster does not lay flat, so putty will be added to give it a more natural look.

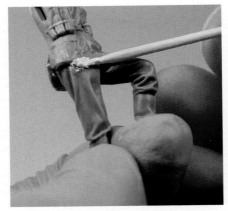

To fill the seams on the plastic figure I use Deluxe Materials Perfect Putty, applying a small amount using a toothpick.

I then use a damp paintbrush to smooth the putty, creating a smooth finish.

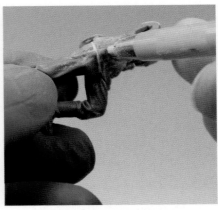

Once the putty dries, I use a fiberglass brush to remove excess putty from the surrounding areas.

After completing this process, it is important to remove any small pieces of broken fiberglass. I do this with an old electric toothbrush.

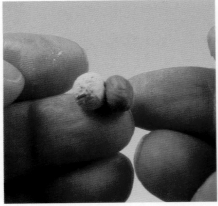

To fill seams on the resin figure I use Aves Apoxie Sculpt. Again, since this is a two-part putty, you must mix equal parts so that it will harden. Mix the parts with a twisting motion until the mix is a uniform grayish white.

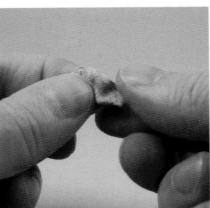

Once the putty is mixed, add a small amount to the seam. I use a homemade tool, a paintbrush that has been sanded to form a rounded point, to press the putty into the seam.

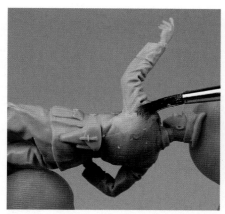

Once the putty is in place, use a moistened paintbrush to help smooth the putty. If you do a good job here you will not have to sand it smooth later.

Once the putty has been smoothed and left to sit for 10 to 15 minutes, I use a hobby knife to carefully add the seam that was missing from the back of the uniform's coat.

2.4 Adding Pins

There are a few reasons to add pins to a figure. The main one is to secure it to a base once you are finished. If you were to just attach it using glue, the chance of it getting knocked over or falling off is greater than if it is pinned. Pinning is also helpful because it makes it easier to hold the figure for painting.

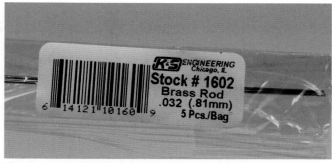

There are several options for pins. I have used brass rod and even paper clips. Here, I use .032 inch brass rod.

I use a wooden-handled jeweler's pin vise to hand-drill parts on my figures or accessory parts. I prefer this to a motor tool because I can better control the speed and depth.

I use my pin vise with the proper drill bit to make a hole in the figure's heel.

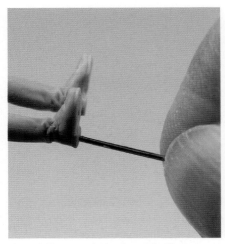  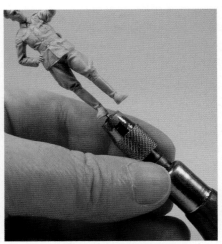

Then drill up to a little above the figure's ankle. Once I have the correct depth, I insert the brass rod with a small amount of super glue to secure it in the foot. I also add a drop of Zip Kicker to speed curing.

Once the rod is secured, and leaving enough room to hold it and pin to it to a base, I use wire cutters to cut the rod at the desired length.

The figure is now pinned and ready for additional work.

2.5 Enhancing Details, Adding Decals, and Photo-etch

There will be times when you can, or will need to, add additional items to a figure to enhance it. This could involve adding photo-etch (PE), brass rods, or decals.

Many companies offer aftermarket products to help achieve a more detailed effect. These require a little prep work and patience, but in the end are worth it.

To make the Germans look better here I used Aber German helmets, liners, and chin straps (No. 35A69) PE parts, a brass rod, and Archer Dry Transfers for the shoulder and collar boards, along with other patches and parts. Much care is needed with PE parts.

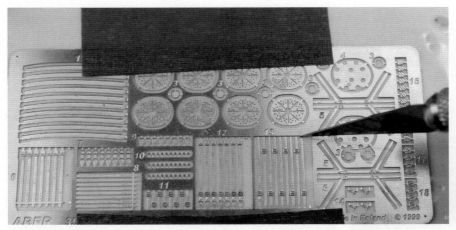 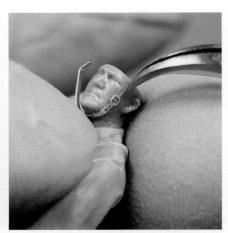

I taped the Aber set to a small piece of tile to keep the thin PE secure, as it is easily bent. Taping to tile adds strength to avoid bending when I use my hobby knife to remove parts from the fret. When removing the part try to get as close as possible to the part so that you do not leave a burr. If you happen to have a small burr, use either a file or sandpaper to gently remove it. Be careful!

Once the chin strap was removed, I gently bent it around the figure's head to form the desired shape. Once I had the shape, I add a small drop of super glue to the side/temple area of the head, then using tweezers I attach the chinstrap to the opposite side of the head, adding another drop of super glue.

I use a toothpick to bend the other side of the chinstrap down onto the top of the head.

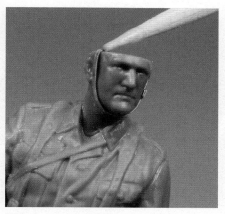

With the chinstrap in place, I add an additional drop of superglue to the top of the head, then add a drop of Zip Kicker to speed curing.

The helmet has been temporarily added to check its fit. The fit is correct. Now it's time to prime and paint.

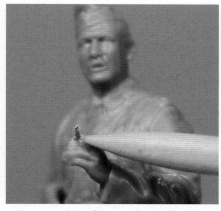

I also wanted this figure to be holding a cigarette, so I used a small drill bit to drill between the fingers before a small thin brass rod is placed between them, cut, and super-glued in place.

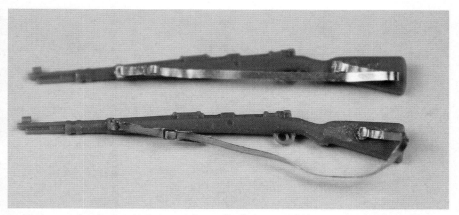

I added one other item to improve realism, rifle slings. I used Aber's Belts and Straps (No. 35A123). These were applied as previously described using super glue.

Here are the rifles with the PE slings and buckles added. Adding these slings is tedious, but patience pays off in the long run.

Ch. 3

PAINTING EYES, FLESH

Good brush, right colors help eyes, flesh tones look realistic

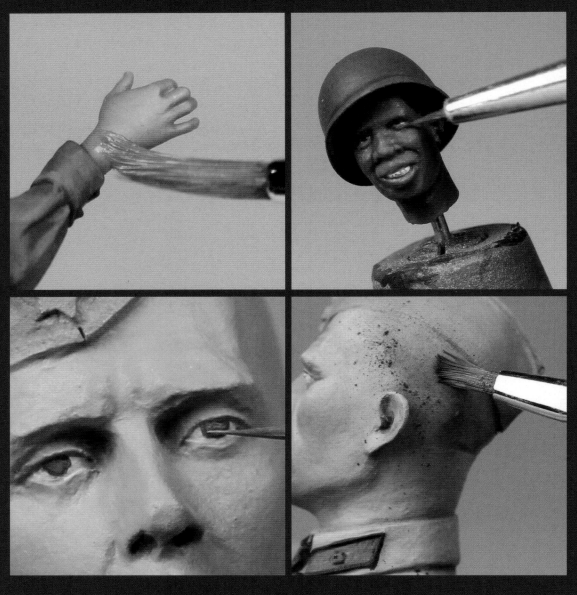

Skin isn't just tan or brown, and eye "whites" aren't just white. Blending colors that accurately reflect natural colors is what makes a figure seem realistic. With eyes, you must consider where the individual figure will be looking, and with skin you'll need to master highlights and shadows.

3.1 Painting Eyes

1/35 SCALE

For years I heard that one of the hardest things about painting faces was getting the eyes right. This can be true, and daunting, but if you use a good brush, proper lighting, and properly thinned paint you can get the results that you are looking for. This may require several attempts, but don't give up or get frustrated, just learn from your mishaps and keep trying.

When I first began painting miniatures more than 30 years ago, I constantly made mistakes, just like I do today. The key is to remember to have fun and enjoy yourself.

If you find yourself getting frustrated, take a look at some of your prior work. I keep the figure at left on my workbench, right in front of me, as a reminder that with practice my figures will get better. I'm still never fully satisfied with my work, but I try daily to improve from my last project.

When painting the eyes in this scale I try to see what the facial expression will look like or how the face/eyes are sculpted. Are the eyes wide open in a shock type of gaze, or are they looking off in a certain direction, or staring straight ahead.

Here you will see several 1/35 examples of the eyes looking in different directions.

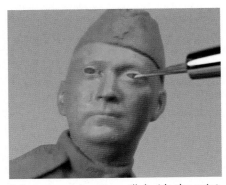

A figure's eye direction will decide the paint application. In this scale I generally paint the whole eye socket with Vallejo Burnt Umber (No. 70.941) or Chocolate Brown (No. 70.872) to start. You can touch up any area with the base flesh mixture if needed at this time. Then, using Vallejo Model Color Green Gray (No. 70.971), apply a small dot only to the side of the eyes away from where the figure will be looking. Here the dots (which will appear white) are applied to the left side of each eye, creating the effect of the eyes looking to the right.

The eyes have been completed here, and you can see that adding the dots of "white" (Green Gray) gives the face some personality and conveys where the figure's attention is at the moment.

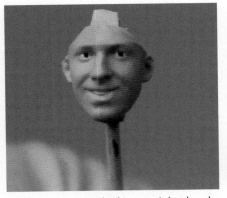

If a figure's eyes are looking straight ahead, I use Green Gray as the "whites" of the eyes. This color has a slight gray tone and gives the illusion of white without being too white. I never use pure white; it looks unnatural. One possible substitute is Vallejo Basic Skintone (No. 70.815). This is a slightly pinkish color that I have also used.

The last example is for creating what appear to be squinting eyes. Here, I leave the whole eye socket Burnt Umber or Chocolate Brown, but make sure that I shape the upper and lower eyelids with a flesh highlight color to suggest that the eyes are squinting. This highlight color will be one or two of the highlight shades that we will use, or have used, for highlighting the entire face.

TIP If you find your paint drying too fast on the tip of your brush, or you can't seem to get it to flow properly, wet your brush with Vallejo Glaze Medium (No. 70.596). This will help the paint flow more evenly off your brush.

TIP At times I may paint the whole eye socket with the "whites" (Green Grey) before adding Burnt Umber or Chocolate Brown to the corners. See what works best for you or what feels most comfortable.

LARGE-SCALE EYES

Example 1: Red Army Junior Lieutenant (1941), Barbarossa

For painting larger scale eyes, as in a 1/16 scale bust, more detail is required. You will need to paint the conjunctiva (whites of the eye), the iris, and the pupils. Plus you'll have to paint the eye socket's upper and lower sections.

To paint this Red Army officer's eyes, I used a No. 0 Tamiya Modeling Brush Pro (No. 87172). Another option is a detail brush from ZEM Brushes.

First, paint the upper eyelid with Vallejo German Camo Black Brown (No. 70.822). Then for the whites of the eyes I use a mixture of Vallejo Green Gray + Citadel Cadian Fleshtone.

Next, carefully place the iris in the center of each eye, starting by making a small dot, then working to each side of it to build the correct shape. I wanted to give this guy greenish eyes, so the base was Vallejo German Extra Dark Green (No. 70.896).

For realism I then give a lighter layer to the iris, using Vallejo German Field Gray (No. 70.181), making a U-shape on the bottom of the iris.

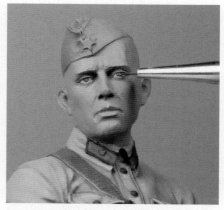

Layering colors is key, so I follow with a lighter, slightly smaller U-shape to the iris. This is German Field Gray mixed with a small amount of the Green Gray. After adding the U-shape at the bottom, I slightly extend it up along the sides of the iris.

Finally, I add a pupil/dot using Scale 75 Flat Black (No. SC-00). To finish the eyes, I add a small bit of catch or reflective light to the side of each eye using Green Gray. If needed, apply any clean up touches to the eyes' whites now.

3.2 Painting Flesh and Hands

LARGE-SCALE WHITE FLESH

I continue to use the Red Army officer to demonstrate effective flesh painting, which can require several approaches in this scale. First, remember that because of its size, very thin layers of paint will be needed to avoid noticeable brush strokes. To achieve this you'll need to use a brush big enough to get the job done. Second, you will need to use less stark highlights or shadows to create a realistic look.

The flesh base coat is Citadel Cadian Fleshtone + Vallejo Brown Sand (No. 70.876). Apply the basecoat in several thin layers with a No. 2 brush. It's important to end up with a smooth application around the head. To help speed the process I use my hair dryer to dry the head between each coat.

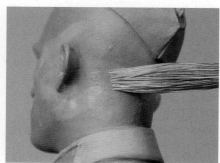

Here you see that the layers are thin and that previous layers are still not fully covering the figure's head. I can't say this enough, but when working with acrylics, it will require many layers to create a proper skin texture.

Here the flesh base coat is complete and the whites of the eyes also have been applied. I will finish the eyes next, before applying any highlights and shadows. By doing the eyes first I can correct any mistakes in the base coat at this stage.

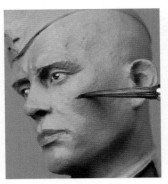

Next, a thin glaze of Vallejo Model Color Transparent Red (No. 70.934) is applied in the cheeks and bottom lip. This is thin enough that it gives the impression of there being life in the flesh.

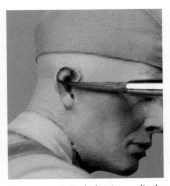

Transparent Red also is applied in and on the ears. This gives these areas depth and a more lifelike appearance.

A mix of Citadel Bugman's Glow + Vallejo Burnt Red (No. 70.814) is then applied in the shadow areas (around the nostrils, under the eyes, chin, and in laugh lines. This mixture of colors helps create depth and simulate blood vessels beneath these areas.

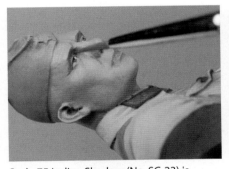

Scale 75 Indian Shadow (No. SC-23) is applied above the eye/under the brow. This area is usually darker and this color is not too stark, so it looks realistic.

Now it's time to add the first highlight mixture using the base + Citadel Cadian Fleshtone. Apply this to highlight the top of the nose, cheekbones, upper lip, nostrils, top of the ears, forehead, etc. Look in the mirror, or at other people, and see where the light and shiny parts are on most faces. Another good source is magazine photos of people's faces.

The next highlight mixture goes on the same areas. It's a mixture of Cadian Fleshtone + Vallejo Beige Red (No. 70.804). Remember to keep this mixture thin, not runny, and apply many layers (5 to 7 may do it) until you have achieved the look you want. Note too that you bring this highlight to the edges of the shadow areas, helping blend the two.

The final highlight is applied to the extreme top of each highlighted area. This is accomplished by applying thin layers of a mix of Beige Red + Vallejo Basic Skintone (No. 70.815).

With the flesh completed I do one more thing with the figure or bust. I hold the figure, then turn my back to the light source to see if I've gotten the correct number of shadows and highlights to bring the figure to life.

ADDING STUBBLE

Adding stubble to a figure can be accomplished using oil paints, acrylics, or pastels.

In the case of the Red Army officer's bust I opted to use pastels because I feel that I have better control of pastels vs. acrylics or oils. I used "soft" color pastels that I found in the art department of my local Walmart. These were not very dark or vibrant compared with other sets I own.

Adding stubble with pastels requires you to take a knife blade or sandpaper and scrape across the pastel stick. Once you have a small pile of pastel dust, take a soft brush and apply it to the desired areas using a soft scrubbing motion.

Continue working around the area and then blow off any excess dust, but do NOT rub it off or you will create a needless mess.

Once the stubble is completed you must seal it to keep the stubble from rubbing off if touched. I seal pastels with Krylon Matte Finish. I like using it because it does not leave the stubble area shiny.

BLACK FLESH AND HANDS

Painting darker flesh is remarkably like that of painting a lighter flesh tone in application, but requires the use of different colors to help bring the flesh to life. The other challenge is to get enough contrast without making the flesh look too stark, unnatural, or lifeless.

The head has been cleaned and primed as described in the introduction to acrylic paints and primers. A base coat of Scale 75 Bosh Chestnut (No. SFG-35) is then applied in several thin layers.

With the eyes completed as described earlier, add a mixture of Vallejo Violet Red (No. 70.812) + Scale 75 Flat Black (No. SC-00) under the eyes' bags and to the underside of the brow. This separates the eyes from the bottom eye lid, brow, and cheeks.

A lighter application of the Violet Red + Flat Black mixture is then applied under the chin, along the jawline, around the nostrils and laugh lines.

That's followed by a highlight mixture of the base color + Scale 75 Mars Orange (No. SC-39) applied to the bottom eyelids.

The same highlight mixture is then applied to the nostrils and tip of the nose.

The highlight mix also is applied to the cheekbones, upper lip, and chin. Gradually lighten this mixture, adding more Mars Orange, and apply it to the same areas as the previous highlight mix. The highest highlights require a small amount of Scale 75 War Front Sahara Sand (No. SW-36) mixed in.

A glaze of Violet Red can then be applied to the hollows of the cheeks to bring the face to life. The same glaze also should be applied to the bottom lip.

The completed face now seems more lifelike and exhibits more character with the additional colors added to the highlights.

HANDS

The hands are sometimes overlooked when painting a figure. But if given additional time and attention, hand detail will help create a more lifelike appearance in your figures.

First, the hands are base-coated with Scale 75 Bosch Chestnut (No. SFG-35). Around the cuffs and between the fingers a mid-dark mixture of Vallejo Violet Red + Scale 75 Flat Black is applied.

An initial highlight is then applied to the top of the hand, along the fingers and knuckles using the base color + Scale 75 Mars Orange.

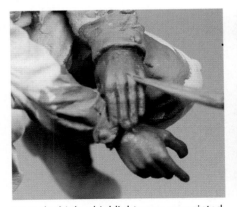

Next, the higher highlight areas are painted using the base + Scale 75 War Front Sahara Sand as in the face. The goal is to be subtle, but also to give the hands a little color to appear more lifelike.

The final step involves creating fingernails. To do this I use Scale 75 Blackert Brown (No. SFG-40), but apply it extremely carefully to the top tips of the fingers.

1/35 SCALE WHITE FLESH AND HANDS

FLESH

Throughout this book you will see many different figures that I have painted, and their flesh tones will be similar, but from time to time I will adjust the flesh mixtures. Mostly the figures have been painted with my usual flesh mixture of Citadel Cadian Flesh, AK Interactive Mahogany Brown (No. AK11106), Vallejo Beige Red (No. 70.804), Vallejo Basic Skintone (No. 70.815), and Scale 75 Indian Shadow (No. SC-23).

Example 1: Russian Soldier

The first Caucasian flesh example is the Russian soldier from my "Berlin Raising the Flag" vignette. I chose him because his face is full of character and it gave me the chance to paint a head without hair, thanks to his cap. First, I base coat his flesh with a mixture of Citadel Cadian Flesh and AK Interactive Mahogany Brown (No. AK11106).

I then use Mahogany Brown with a small amount of the base flesh mixture to draw in the creases that form from outside the nostril down to the outside of the upper lip's corner. You'll notice I've already painted the eyes as described earlier in the eye painting section.

Using the same mixture, I then add a shadow under the bottom lip as well as under the chin. The figure has a double chin, so this shadow mixture also was applied there.

Continue with the same mixture below the eye bags and above the eyes to accentuate the deep recesses. On some faces I use Scale 75 Indian Tone to darken these areas, but not in this case.

Next, add highlights, beginning with the upper lip. For this I use the base flesh tone + more Cadian Flesh.

I continue adding highlights to other areas on the face, including the brow. These are made by applying layers of Cadian Flesh, Cadian Flesh + Beige Red, and lastly pure Beige Red. Remember to keep the paint thin when adding layers. Do *not* use heavy amounts of paint.

Here is the wet palette I use with various mixes I'll apply in layers. Note these are thin but controllable colors.

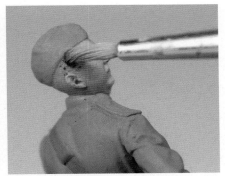

Since this figure's head does not have exposed hair, I create stubble with pastels near the hat's edge. I applied them, as previously described, with a stiff brush.

Here the face and stubble are complete, excess pastels removed and the head sealed with Krylon Matte finish.

Example 2: German Soldier

Like most of the figures I paint, this soldier's base coat is a mixture of Citadel Cadian Flesh and AK Interactive Mahogany Brown.

Because I wanted this soldier to appear more weary than most, I applied several thinned glazes of Vallejo Transparent Red (No. 70.934) around the eyes and in the hollows of his cheeks. This color is very strong so use it sparingly and well-thinned.

Next I apply a mixture of Mahogany Brown + Scale 75 Indian Shadow (SC-23) into the folds of the nose creases. This also is applied along the chinstrap and under the chin.

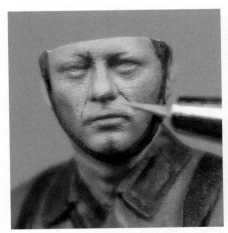

Next apply 5 to 7 thin highlight layers of base + Cadian Flesh to the top lip, chin, cheekbones, eye bags, and Adam's apple. Transition to pure Cadian Flesh. Then add a little Vallejo Beige Red to the Cadian Flesh in creases near the nose to create depth.

The brightest highlights are applied to the tip of the nose, each nostril, highest cheekbone areas near the eyes and the chin. These are a mixture of Cadian Flesh, Beige Red + a small amount of Vallejo Sunny Skintone (No. 70.845).

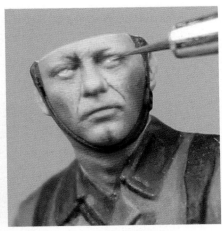

In previous examples I painted the eye sockets with either Chocolate Brown or Burnt Umber, but here I used Vallejo Green Gray.

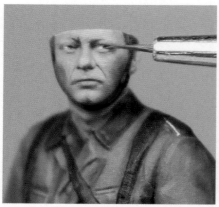 

With the whites of the eyes painted I added a small dot of Chocolate Brown to the left corner of each eye to give the appearance the soldier is looking to his left.

I thought I was a finished, but look closely and you'll see I added slightly darker shadows to the inside corners of the brow by the nose to give the face extra character.

HANDS

When painting hands you need to consider the angle or their position to determine what highlights and shadows are needed. Each hand may have a somewhat similar area for highlights or shadows, but their position could call for a slight variation. In this example I use the flesh mixture of Citadel Cadian Flesh, AK Interactive Mahogany Brown (No. AK11106), Vallejo Beige Red (No. 70.804), Vallejo Basic Skintone (No. 70.815), Scale 75 Indian Shadow (No. SC-23), and Scale 75 Flat Black (SC-00).

 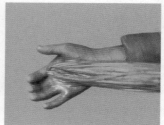  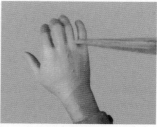

The hands were previously base coated with the flesh mixture of Cadian Flesh + Mahogany Brown. Here I added more Mahogany Brown to the base, as this hand will be pointing upward, so I applied a shadow in the wrist.

The hand also will be pressed up against the boot of another figure, so this requires a shadow on the hand's palm. For that I add even more Mahogany Brown to the mix than was previously applied to the wrist.

With the hand pointing up, highlighting is needed in the webbing between the thumb and index finger. Apply several layers of varying highlight mixes of the base coat with more Cadian Fleshtone added, then pure Cadian Fleshtone, and lastly a mix of Cadian Fleshtone + Beige Red.

Next add highlights to each knuckle and the fingers. I use Cadian Fleshtone and then a mix of Cadian Fleshtone + Beige Red. This helps shape the hand, taking a flat looking piece of plastic or resin and giving it depth.

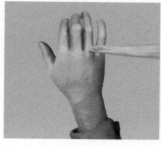  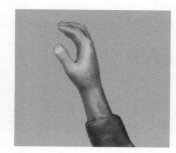

The last highlight involves adding just a small amount of basic Skintone mixed with Beige Red for extreme highlights, such as on the knuckles.

To separate each finger from the other you'll want to add a darker color that will not be too noticeable but creates visual separation. I have found Indian Tone works best for this basic application. If needed you can then mix a small amount of black to create a dark wine color, which is more pleasing to the eye.

Finally, add a fingernail to each finger. I find it best to use Basic Skintone mixed with a small amount of Vallejo Red Beige. Apply to each finger, remembering to leave a small amount of flesh at the tip of each. The hands are complete.

32

PAINTING EQUIPMENT

From head to toe, fine detailing makes a figure seem more authentic

Here we'll look at detailing boots, helmets, and weapons. There were several types of boots worn by the men and women of WWII. I will highlight the ones more commonly used throughout the war and explain how I achieve various textures and finishes. For ease of reference I'll break these down by countries, but the examples can be used with other versions not discussed here.

4.1 Boots

US M-1944 OVERSHOE

Early in WWII, the most-desired boot for U.S. Army soldiers was the M-1944 Overshoe. This featured a rubberized cotton upper with a flexible rubber sole and four metal buckles. These were great in the snow and mud and afforded added protection to the soldiers' feet.

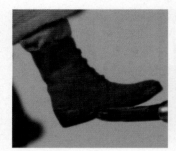

Begin by giving the boots a base coat of Scale 75 Flat Black (No. SC-00) plus Scale 75 Graphene Gray (No. SC-58) for the upper section and Vallejo Flat Black (No. 70.950) for the soles.

Here Graphene Gray is added to the base coat. This was then applied to the highlight areas, gradually adding more of the gray to the mix before applying it to the highest areas.

Vallejo Flat Black is then added to the base mixture and applied to the shadow areas on the boots' upper sections.

Scale 75's Inktense Black (No. SC-79) is my choice for the boots' buckles.

US M-1943 COMBAT BOOT

The M-1943 was first approved in 1943 and was mass produced during the later stages of the war. By 1945 it had been heavily issued to all troops overseas. It was also called the double buckle boot because of the boot's unique double-buckled upper section.

Here start with a base coat of Vallejo Panzer Aces Leather Belt (No. 70.312) + a small amount of Scale 75 Flat Black applied to the boots' lower section.

For the upper sections, use a base coat of AK Interactive Red Brown (No. AK11434) + a small amount of Scale 75 Flat Black.

Next apply a darker version of the base coat (adding small amounts of Flat Black) to all the boot seams and folds.

To create more depth and realism, highlights need to be applied to all raised areas. I dab with the brush and start with more AK Red Brown, then gradually add AK Deep Orange (No. AK 11080) to the mix.

As with the boots' lower section, add a darker shadow version of the base to all folds on the upper boot. For highlights, start by adding a little Red Brown to the base and gradually increase to just Red Brown. For a lighter highlight add a touch of AK Deep Orange to the Red Brown.

To set off the buckles, I paint them using a mix of Vallejo Burnt Umber (No. 70.941) + Vallejo Model Color Brass (No. 70.801).

GERMAN

German soldiers wore several types of boots. Early- to mid-war the German enlisted soldiers were issued M39 Jack Boots, sometimes referred to as Marschstiefel, or marching boots, by the Germans. These were common among the German infantry and stormtroopers.

These boots were made of leather and dyed black. They also included pull straps, leather soles, iron heels, and hobnails. I have found several ways to approach painting certain German items, including these boots.

Here are two examples of how I approach German boots.

Example 1: Base Coat

I create a base coat by mixing paints from the Andrea Black Paint set (ACS-02) and Scale 75 Black and White set. Here I use Andrea Black No. 6 + Scale 75 Graphene Gray.

Next, gently dry-brush the boot with Graphene Gray, using a soft, flat brush. It's important to use a minimal amount of paint to do this. The dry-brushing isn't simply to add highlights but to help bring out boot details.

Here you can see that there is just a minimal amount of paint on the boots from the dry-brushing.

Highlights accented by dry-brushing now need more attention. I take the base coat and gradually add several layers of Graphene Gray to highlighted areas.

Next, enhance the shadows using Vallejo Flat Black in the creases and other shadowy areas. I chose the Vallejo brand here because it dries to more of a satin finish than other brands. This helps give the boot a livelier look.

Here are the boots after highlights and shadows have been applied.

Then add weathering to the boot using Vallejo Mahogany Brown (No. 70.846), adding dabs here and there to simulate a worn and weathered look. The casting had a natural looking defect in the right boot's toe, so I opted to leave it and weather it like the boot had been damaged in battle.

Here are the finished boots with highlights, shadows, and weathering completed.

In this example I create a base coat of AK Smoke Black (No. AK11028) + AK Leather (No. AK11110) for the boots.

Next, mix more Leather into the base. Then add more water to this mixture to make it more of a tint before applying this as a controlled glaze to all highlighted areas. This step helps blend the colors.

Gradually add more of the Leather and then apply this to the boots' toes. This simulates a worn, scuffed look.

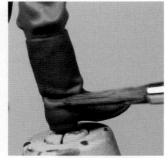

Follow that by gradually adding Leather to areas such as the boot sides that would naturally crease and show wear from excessive use.

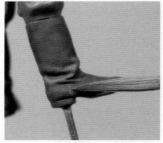

Boots also have seams where the different leather sections are sewn together. To simulate this I add pure Leather mixed with a small amount of Citadel Mournfang Brown (No. 640909), a reddish brown.

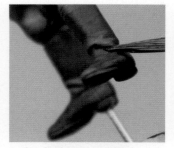

In the shadow areas, apply more Smoke Black, and in the deepest areas use Scale 75 Flat Black to visually create depth.

Then use the same Flat Black to paint along the soles and heels of the boots.

The boots are complete, except for a last step completed once the whole figure is painted. That's when I apply Vallejo Satin Varnish (No. 70.522) to the boots' upper sections.

4.2 Helmets and Web Belts

HELMETS

M1 helmets were used by the United States in WWII and up until 1985. During WWII, the helmet weighed about 2.85 pounds (1.29kg), including the chin strap and liner. Not surprisingly, the color was Olive Drab. This had varying hues depending on whether it was newly issued, had been worn in the weather, or simply was painted with a different batch of paint.

Here I apply a base coat of Vallejo Model Color Brown Violet (No. 70.887) + Scale 75 Flat Black. You can airbrush or hand brush several layers. I hand brushed, but remember to use thin applications. I also used a hair dryer to speed the drying process between each layer.

For the chin straps on the front and back of the helmet, I use a mixture of Vallejo Mahogany Brown + a small amount of Scale 75 Flat Black.

Then I gradually add more Mahogany Brown to the mix, paying attention to the top edges. Next, I add a touch of Scale 75 Chink Orange (No. SFG-37) to the top edges for a strong highlight. I also add more Flat Black to the original helmet mixture and outline the strap's edges against the helmet. This gives the chin straps a 3-D look.

WEB BELT

When painting a figure, it is sometimes the little things that help make it look more realistic or can make your figure pop in a display or diorama. This can be as simple as painting web belts or other gear accurately. Sometimes we get the "important" parts of a figure painted, then rush to have it on the base, neglecting the little things. Here is an example of painting a web belt for a US soldier.

BASE COAT

For this I create a base coat of Scale 75 War Zone Grau (No. SW-29) + Scale 75 War Zone Pale Earth (No. SW-34).

I then add the metal sections to the straps using Scale 75 Inktense Black (No. SC-79). I do this now so that if I happen to get any on a surrounding area, I still have my base coat handy to make necessary corrections.

Using my ZEM 10/0 brush I use No. 6 from my Andrea Brown paint set (ACS-013) to separate all the straps from each other and the overcoat.

Then start adding shadows to the webbing using a mixture of the base + Scale 75 Pale Earth. You can continue adding more shadows to the webbing by increasing the Pale Earth. Subsequent shadows were created using plain Pale Earth and the deepest areas were a mixture of Pale Earth and Andrea Brown No. 6.

Next, I add highlights to the slings and ammo pouches using the base mix with a little War Zone Grau added to the mix. But add the Grau gradually until just Grau is used for the highest highlights.

4.3 Weapons

Your miniature's weapons require the same attention to detail that you give your figures. Like on the figures, there should be highlights and shadows to various areas on the weapons. This attention to detail will enhance the overall look of your figure.

Most of the time when painting weapons you'll have to deal with two types of materials, the metal of a barrel and other metal parts, along with wooden areas, such as stocks and buttstocks.

Here are a few examples on how to paint a figure's weapons.

METAL PARTS
Example 1

This example will be using an airbrush and metallic paints. The next example on page 39 will be old school, using graphite.

First, clean up seams, remove any flash, and be careful as you are removing the weapons from the carrier. Follow with a smooth primer coat, either via a spray can, brush, or airbrush.

Next, mix an equal amount of Scale 75 Black Metal (No. SC-83) and Scale 75 Intense Black (No. SC-79) and airbrush it on all metal areas. It is OK to brush this on. However, remember to keep this mixture thin and allow each layer to dry between applications.

Adding shadows to the metal creates realism. Add them around the bands on the barrel, the areas where the metal meets the wood, and along seams created by metal areas touching each other. Apply Scale 75 Flat Black with a pointed Size 0 brush.

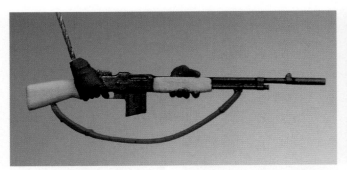

Here we see the shadow areas completed, adding depth to the gun's barrel, trigger and clip.

Lastly, you'll want to apply random highlights to the metal areas. They should be random because the initial base metal coat already has a slight shine that causes natural highlights. I apply Scale 75 Black Metal to the top of the barrel, the sight, areas along the edge of the mid-section, and along the magazine's edges.

WOODEN AREAS

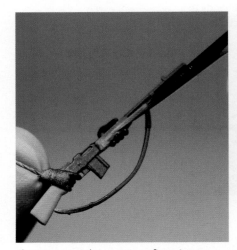

The gun's wooden areas are first given a base coat of 3 parts Scale 75 Braun Brown (No. SW-06) + 1 part Scale 75 Rotbraun Primer Red (No. SW-03) using a Size 0 brush.

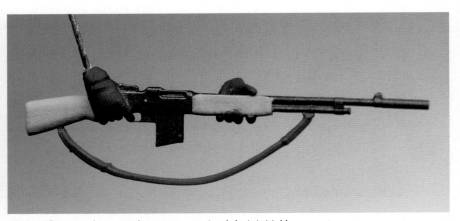

All the rifle's wooden parts have now received their initial base coat.

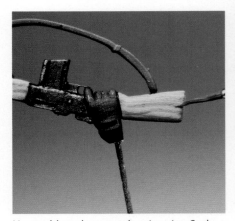

Next, add random wood grain using Scale 75 Rotbraun Primer Red with a pointed Size 0 brush. This does not have to be precise, just a few controlled squiggly lines.

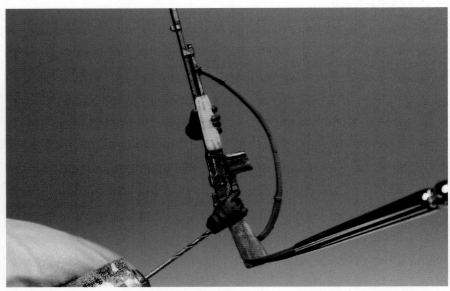

I then apply a thin glaze using Scale 75 Inktense Chestnut (No. SC-81) on all the wooden areas. To create the glaze I add just a little water to the ink to thin it. It's key to apply extremely thin layers, as this ink is extremely powerful.

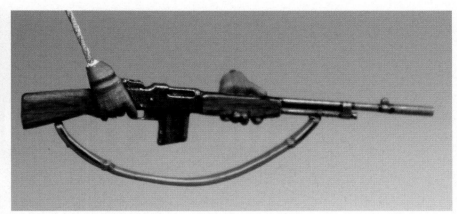

Adding darker grains to the wood increases realism. I use Scale 75 Flat Black to apply random dark thin lines in the wooden areas, again using a fine pointed Size 0 brush.

Now the weapon is complete.

Example 2

Here we'll use the older method of applying graphite to a weapon. First, I use a base coat of Scale 75 Flat Black on the machine gun.

Follow that by rubbing a No. 2 pencil on a piece of sandpaper to create a small mound of graphite.

Next, load a soft brush with graphite by rubbing it into the mound on the sandpaper. Then rub or scrub the brush on the gun's metal areas. Excess graphite will get on the figure, but *don't* rub it off – blow it away.

It's safe to now paint the wooden areas with a mixture of Mahogany Brown and Flat Black. Highlight these areas by adding more Mahogany Brown and more Flat Black to the mixture to create the necessary shadows.

Here we see the completed weapon. Note that I've put a little extra work into highlighting the gun's higher metal areas by gently running the point of the pencil across the extreme highlighted areas.

CONVERSIONS

Making figures fit your scene by rearranging or adding parts

Sometimes a figure seems nearly perfect for a diiorama or vignette you're creating, but it needs something extra – maybe a new head, new hand, or arms posed differently than that original figure. You can borrow those parts from another figure and convert your figure to better fit the scene. Here are several ways I alter figures to fit my modeling needs.

5.1 Changing Heads and Arms

A friend of mine, Jerry, told me he had several spare Tiger tank parts, so I asked if he could make me a cupola and cut it so that I could use it as a setting for a figure I planned. He came through big time. What he made served as a great prop for the figure and the idea that I had imagined. Now I had to make the figure's pose fit the scene.

I bought Tamiya's 1/35 scale Wehrmacht Tank Crew Set (No: 35354) with the intention of using a few of the crew in a diorama. But I really liked one figure and wanted to use him in a single figure setting. This is his final configuration.

To start this conversion, I took the selected figure from the set and assembled it as I described in Chapter 2, with one exception, not gluing the head on.

The figure has great details, but because it is injection-molded, some areas are not as crisp as I would like, especially around the belt.

I took my hobby knife and slowly removed some of the excess plastic, creating a separation between the body and belt.

After removing the excess plastic, I used sanding foam to begin smoothing the areas I'd just scraped, being careful not to damage surrounding details.

Next, I used modeling glue on the areas I had scribed. The glue will dissolve or melt away any loose plastic, helping smooth those areas.

Here we can see the completed belt area, cleaner and more realistic.

I found the replacement head I was looking for from Alpine Miniatures. I felt its expression and details would enhance my project.

I needed to work on this area, where the elbow would be underneath the jacket sleeve. I also temporarily added the head to the body using a pin and super glue, as described in Chapter 2.

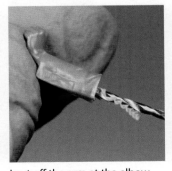

I cut off the arm at the elbow, then drilled a hole in the base of the forearm.

The same process was repeated to the portion of the upper arm still attached to the body.

I inserted a brass rod using super glue in each of the corresponding holes. The arm was then bent and maneuvered into the desired position.

That left quite a gap, so I used super glue to fill it, accelerating the process by adding a drop of accelerator to the glue.

NOTE The super glue, which was added to the sculpting tools and sanded smooth, helps prevent the wet putty from sticking to the tool.

Next, I needed to remove some of the plastic to get a proper surface so that I could add putty as a filler.

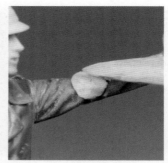

Adding a small amount of Aves Apoxie Sculpt to the area, I use my finger to move it to the correct position. Then I use one of my sculpting tools (a sanded down old paintbrush coated with super glue) to smooth it.

I then use my sculpting tool to make the desired folds in the figure's sleeve.

Follow this up by using a damp paintbrush to smooth the putty. This helps alleviate a lot of unnecessary sanding later.

I then add some leftover Verlinden photo-etched badges from my parts box to the figure's uniform because the plastic badges' details were soft, lacking defined shape.

I also though the figure would look better pointing than giving the "halt" sign with his hand, so I removed the hand. Using my snippers, I cut as close to the coat sleeve as possible without damaging the sleeve.

The sleeve was then drilled out using a drill bit almost the size of the sleeve, but being careful to not damage the area.

I chose a pointing left hand from the 1/35 scale hand set from Scientific Models. I thought this hand with the finger's position would create the impression that the figure was pointing at something important.

Again I drilled a hole, this time in the hand, and a brass wire was inserted and super glued in place. Once it had cured, I glued it into the arm.

Because I decided on a different hand, this would require the arm's sleeve to have different folds than previously sculpted. I removed a bit of the excess putty and plastic, then resculpted the area.

Finally the figure is sanded and primed to check if it is ready for painting or if there are imperfections I may have missed.

BRITISH UNIFORMS

From officers to soldiers, nailing the British look takes patience

I received an early copy of the Field Marshal Bernard "Monty" Montgomery figure from Tarter Miniatures, a 75mm resin kit. It is an awesome resemblance to the portrait that was painted by Reginald Hennery Lewis (1894-1973) and hangs in the Royal Regiment of Fusiliers Museum in Warwick, England. The figure is wearing his officers' uniform and an oversized leather coat. Here's how I painted it. That, and more here, applies to various British WWII uniforms.

6.1 General's Leather Coat, Fur

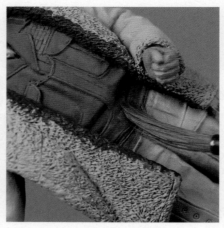

For the base coat on the general's tunic I used Vallejo English Uniform (No. 70.921) + a small amount of Vallejo Chocolate Brown (No. 70.872). This was applied with several thin coats, and the process was sped up by using a hair dryer between each layer.

Here I add more Chocolate Brown and make a controlled wash that flows into the bottom area to create shadows. I do this now, but go back into the highlight and shadow areas later. This gives the fabric more depth and variation.

Next, combine the Chocolate Brown with a small amount of Vallejo German Cam Black Brown (No. 70.822) and apply it in the deepest shadow areas and along seams.

Adding highlights begins by mixing the base mixture and a small amount of Vallejo Desert Yellow (No. 70.977). Apply this in thin layers along all high sections of the tunic.

To further enhance the highlights, mix in more Desert Yellow to the base, and also add Vallejo Dark Sand (No. 70.847), applying several more layers to the previously highlighted areas.

The tunic is finished, including all highlights, shadows, edging, and lining. The lining should be almost pure (about 95%) Vallejo German Camo Black Brown (No. 70.822) + 5% Chocolate Brown, while the edging should be almost pure (about 95%) Vallejo Dark Sand (No. 70.847) + 5% Desert Yellow (No. 70.977). Adding the lining and edging really helps detailing pop.

To finish this portion of the figure I paint the general's ribbons, using a variety of colors to match his awards. A good pointed brush is needed, plus thinned paints and patience.

BASE COAT

Moving on to the leather overcoat I apply a base of Scale 75 Bosh Chestnut (No. SFG-35) + War Zone Flat Black (No. SW-15). Always apply in thin layers and remember you can cut drying time by using a hair dryer.

Then move on to the fur collar, cuffs, and coat's bottom. The base for the fur is Andrea Base Flesh Set No. 5, but you could substitute Scale 75 Chink Orange (No. SFG-37) or Vallejo Model Color Orange Brown (No. 70.981) + Andrea Brown Set No. 3.

Here you can see the back of the coat and fur have been base coated, but note that even in this first step I try to paint these areas as neatly as possible.

BUCKLE

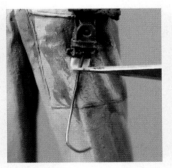

Once everything was base coated, I noticed that my casting's buckle was broken. So I took a small piece of sheet styrene, formed a buckle, and glued it on the leg by the coat's belt area.

I then took a small length of .010 lead wire and super glued it in place on the buckle.

Using a sharp hobby knife, I carefully cut the lead wire to the proper length.

The new buckle is complete. Once painted, it will look just like it was supposed to be there.

HIGHLIGHTS AND SHADOWS

Time to add shadows on the overcoat with a mix of the base coat color with additional black to provide contrast in the shadowy areas, such as the coat's creases.

For deeper shadows, add to the shadow mixture a small amount of Vallejo Model Color Royal Purple (No. 70.810). I use purple instead of black as I feel it adds life to the coat. Just adding more black tends to make the leather look flat.

Highlights are next. I create a mix using the base + more Andrea Flesh No. 5 and apply it to all highlight areas, such as the raised folds of the coat. Instead of brushing it on, try a stippling motion. This gives the coat a worn appearance.

The highest highlights are randomly selected. I used a mix of the earlier highlight mixture + Scale 75 War Zone Desert Yellow (No. SW-31). Again, this process is done randomly and using the stippling application for a worn look.

With leather areas complete, it's time to finish the fur. These areas already have been base coated, as mentioned earlier.

Begin by adding shadows, such as inside the fold of the general's coat. Use the base coat and gradually add Andrea Brown No. 3 until the tone is realistic.

To add more highlights, combine the base mix with Scale 75 Chink Orange, but add it gradually to achieve a more realistic blend.

The last highlights are applied using a stippling motion with the Chink Orange and varying amounts of Vallejo Dark Sand (No. 70.847) to create contrast.

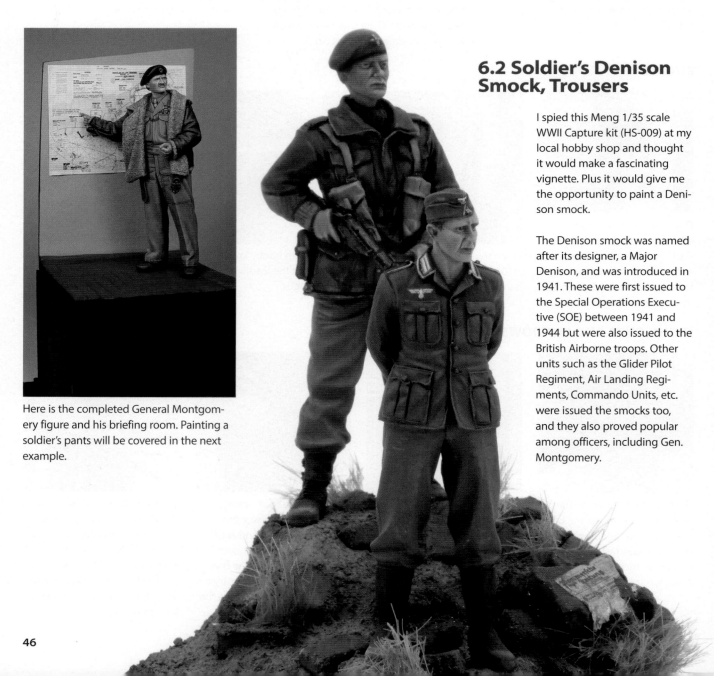

Here is the completed General Montgomery figure and his briefing room. Painting a soldier's pants will be covered in the next example.

6.2 Soldier's Denison Smock, Trousers

I spied this Meng 1/35 scale WWII Capture kit (HS-009) at my local hobby shop and thought it would make a fascinating vignette. Plus it would give me the opportunity to paint a Denison smock.

The Denison smock was named after its designer, a Major Denison, and was introduced in 1941. These were first issued to the Special Operations Executive (SOE) between 1941 and 1944 but were also issued to the British Airborne troops. Other units such as the Glider Pilot Regiment, Air Landing Regiments, Commando Units, etc. were issued the smocks too, and they also proved popular among officers, including Gen. Montgomery.

SMOCK

First, I base coat the British figure's smock using AK Interactive Green Brown (No. AK11126). This has a nice hue and will serve as a great base for the upcoming steps.

Then add Red Brown islands to the smock, using AK Interactive Red Brown (No. AK11434). These are added to the front, back, and each arm. I used a reference photo of a smock to get as close to the shapes and locations of the islands as I could. In addition, I added the splatter/lines that come from the islands.

Adding the green islands is next using AK Interactive Gunship Green (No. AK11150). This looks too bright initially but will be muted in future steps.

To add the green splatter/lines I first thinned the paint and then removed excess paint from the brush. Then I carefully paint the splatter/lines.

Follow that with a thin wash of Vallejo Model Wash Brown (No. 76.513) over the entire smock. Apply it lightly, gradually building it up with several layers. Next, add a small amount of Vallejo Model Wash Black (No. 76.518) to the Brown wash to darken it. Finally, thinly apply this mix over the smock.

Here you can see the results of the wash. It helped blend and darken the smock to create a more realistic worn look.

Apply highlights next using a thin amount of each color, the base, Gunship Green, and Red Brown to randomly add highlights. This helps make each area pop, but will not take away from the overall camouflage look. This process should be done very lightly and randomly.

Finally, the smock is complete after the highlights have been added. You can see it looks a bit glossy from the process, but I next will airbrush Vallejo Matte Medium (No. 70.540), *not* the Matte Varnish, over the areas to correct the gloss problem.

TROUSERS

The soldier's pants, like those of the general earlier, are base-coated with Vallejo English Uniform. Initial shadows have been applied to the necessary areas using the base and a small amount of Vallejo Burnt Umber (No. 70.941).

To shade the areas that require darker shadows, I gradually mix in more Burnt Umber and apply that to the deeper creases.

Because these trousers have a pocket, it is important to outline it to help separate it from the pants leg. Use Burnt Umber by itself to outline the pocket and delineate the seam down the outside of each leg.

Again you can use pure Burnt Umber to create depth in the wrinkles and folds that require a deeper shadow.

To create the initial highlights, mix the English Uniform base with a small amount of AK Interactive Decomposed Flesh (No. AK11058). It is important to keep these layers thin and gradually build them up to create a smooth appearance instead of a stark, non-blended look.

For the highest highlights, the areas that receive the largest amount of light, I will use more of the Decomposed Flesh paint to lighten the look.

Here we see the finished soldier figures on the base, apparently contemplating what will happen next.
KEVIN THOMPSON PHOTO

The kit did not provide a base, so I used an old resin base from my spare parts box. It was the basic shape I had envisioned. I thought it would be more dramatic to have the British soldier standing above the German prisoner, so I used epoxy putty to build up the ground's height, adding bricks and a short section of styrene tubing to the wet putty. Once it was all glued down, I applied Vallejo Earth Textures Dark Brown (No. 26.218) over the base.

UNITED STATES UNIFORMS

coats, field jackets, and overalls require proper highlights and sha

he US Army Winter Coat or Melton Wool Overcoat was originally developed for dress, parade and furlough wear, but during the European winter of 1944-45 it was called into service. Man soldiers relied primarily on this for warmth in the field, not

7.1 GI in Winter Coat

During production of the coats for the war, demand for brass, copper, and bronze was high. These became essential metals that were needed in the production of ordinance, equipment (web gear, buckles, and uniform buttons). To cut metal use, a new type of plastic was used for the coat's buttons.

For this U.S. figure I chose the Scale 75 War Front series kit, Private First Class (Pfc), and used various colors from Scale 75, Vallejo, and Andrea to finish the figure.

BASE COAT

I start with a base coat of Scale 75 US Dark Brown from its Winter Coat set (SSE-066). For smooth coverage I use my airbrush to fully cover the figure. You can get the same results with a brush, but you need to keep the layers thin and use a hair dryer in between each layer to speed drying.

Adding a small amount of the Andrea Brown Paint set's No. 6 (No. ACS-013) to the base, I airbrush the mixture to the bottom of the figure, its deep folds, into the underside of the arms, and in the front where there would be shadows.

With airbrushing complete and the figure dry, you can see the darker areas. In a bit I will come back and enhance these areas.

OUTLINING

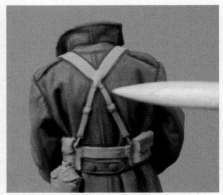

Next, paint around the coat's hems. For this, again use Andrea Brown No. 6, but thin it to an ink consistency. I use a ZEM No. 0 brush to accent the hems.

Note: At this point I also have base coated the web belting and canteen.

Use the same Andrea Brown No. 6 to outline the webbing and the coat's front fold, where the coat overlaps the other side.

Here you can see the outline around the belts on the back and the separation of the belts from the wool coat.

SHADOWS

For shadows I use the base color and gradually add more Andrea Brown No. 6 to the mix. The deeper shadows then receive more Brown No. 6, while I add a small amount of Vallejo Flat Black (No. 70.950) to the mix for the deepest folds.

This deep shadow mix is also used here to separate and show a seam where the sleeves meet the coat's main section.

HIGHLIGHTS

 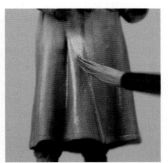

To add highlights, use the base color + Andrea Brown No. 3. This is applied to highlight the top areas of the coat, then gradually build up the highlights by adding more Andrea No. 3 + Scale 75 Blackert Brown (No. SFG-40).

The larger folds on the lower front and back require a little finesse. When using acrylics it is important to either use a thinner amount of paint and gradually build it up, or use some form of slow-drying additive. I used the thinned paint method, gradually building it up. I also used a No. 2 paintbrush here.

EDGING

Next, I want to edge the collar, cuffs, and other areas using a bright color. I chose Scale 75 Blackert Brown. Use the side of your brush and run it along the edges. Doing this helps separate the different areas and give the figure some pop.

The basic colors and detail work on the coat is complete, but I will go back later to add more details and weathering after I finish the web belt.

When complete I attach the figure to a groundwork-coated base with super glue. But there's a bit more to come.

I wanted to add snow to the scene and the figure. You can do this by airbrushing a mist of a water and white glue mix onto the figure and groundwork. Then use AK Interactive snow lightly sprinkled from above using a spatula and tapping the spatula gently. This allows the snow to fall gently and accumulate with a natural appearance.

Now the figure and small vignette are complete, creating the appearance of a wintery foxhole somewhere in Germany.

7.2 Black Soldiers Vignette

The idea for this vignette came when I saw a black and white photo online of two Black soldiers holding artillery rounds along with a basket full of rounds with words on them saying "Happy Easter Hitler." So I began researching and discovered the two soldiers were Technical Sergeant William E. Thomas and Private First-Class Joseph Jackson of the 333rd Field Artillery Battalion. At the time of the photo they were part of the 969th Artillery Battalion, and the picture was taken during the Battle of Remagen, March 10, 1945. I originally set out to sculpt the scene before a friend advised me that there was a kit called Easter Gifts from MIG Productions (No. MP35-416) in 1/35 scale replicating the photo.

The M41 Field Jacket on these figures was common during the war and was issued as Olive Drab No. 2, which is a pale olive color. But over time they would fade and look more like a shade of khaki.

When I dry-fit the soldier and shell I found there was a small gap between the shell and the body of the soldier holding the artillery round. This had to be fixed before I began to paint.

I applied AVES Apoxie Putty to the body, then using a brush I added talcum powder to the wet putty. This helps keep the shell from sticking to the soldier's body.

I then pressed the shell (hands attached) into the wet putty and removed any excess before letting it dry.

The shell was removed after about 3 hours. Because I had used the talcum powder earlier, this process was easily completed.

To help smooth the putty's edges I gently use a small piece of sanding foam. It's important to use a light hand and not damage the putty.

Next, I prime the figure and give it a base coat of AK Interactive's Canvas Tone (No. AK11436), applying it in several thin coats until coverage is complete.

For shadowy areas, mix the base color with an exceedingly small amount of Scale 75 Flat Black.

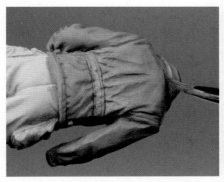

A little blacker shade should be applied to the underside of the collar.

Highlights can then be applied to all the raised areas on the jacket using a mix of the base + AK's Ocher Khaki (No. AK 11422).

The brightest highlights and edging are added last using the highlight mix with varying amounts of Vallejo Model Color Green Gray (No. 70.971) mixed in.

PAINTING TROUSERS

The soldiers' pants first receive a base coat of equal amounts of AK Dark Olive (No. AK 11421) + AK US Olive Base Uniform (No. AK 11433).

For shadow areas I use a darker version of the base coat, adding small amounts of Scale 75 Flat Black to the base color. For seams, add more black to create an even darker shadow mix.

Highlights are applied after gradually adding more U.S. Olive to the base color, eventually ending up only using U.S. Olive. Edging and outer seams are painted using the last step's highlight mix + a small amount of Vallejo Green Gray.

Here the trousers and jacket are complete except for the jacket buttons, which will be painted with AK's Dark Olive.

Both figures complete, here's the finished vignette. I was happy to complete this project, which I had wanted to make for some time.

7.3 Military Police Vignette

For some time I'd had this idea for a vignette portraying US Army Military Policeman somewhere in Germany with a big score of refreshments. I wanted to portray them in the 5th Corps, which was the same that I served in while in Germany as an MP. The title, "Confiscated or Appropriated," came from my time in the military when an officer would ask us MPs, "Where did you get that, or those?" Our answer usually was, "We confiscated it" Or with a smile, "We appropriated it, sir."

The vignettes base came from Italeri's Check Point kit (No. 415) with the Jeep and driver's body coming from a Takom kit (No. TAK2126). I substituted a spare Alpine Miniatures head for the driver's head, and the standing MP also is from Alpine, the WWII US Infantry NSO (No. 35184). I painted both figures the same way, but I will explain the process using the standing MP.

MPs at this time wore brassards or armbands. So before priming the figure I had to sculpt one on the figure's left arm, which I did by rolling out a thin layer of AVES Apoxy Sculpt.

Once I finished the brassard, I decided the figure needed a cigarette in his hand to give him a look of "coolness" or arrogance. So I drilled a small hole between the fingers and inserted a thin brass rod cut to the proper length.

When I paint figures, I like to base coat them in their base colors. I do this because the adjacent colors help frame the area I am working on and will help me achieve a more realistic finish. I applied the base colors in thin layers so as not to cover any of the figure's details. Here's what I used.

COLORS:
Jacket: Vallejo Khaki (No. 70.988) + a dab of Vallejo Burnt Umber (No. 70.941) at approximately a 90%-10% ratio
Collar and Cuffs: AK Field Drab (No. AK 11435) + Vallejo German Camo Black Brown (No. 70.822) at a 40%-60% ratio
Trousers: AK Muddy Brown (No. AK 11120) + Vallejo German Camo Black Brown (No. 70.822) at an 80%- 20% ratio

First, add shadows to the folds, the shallow areas along the sleeves, front/back of the jacket, and the zipper seam. These will not be as dark as deeper folds, except the zipper seam, which later will receive a thin, dark seam. The shadow mix consists of the base coat, but with more Burnt Umber added. It's important to keep these applications extremely thin and to apply several layers vs. one thick layer. This helps in blending colors with adjacent colors.

Next, outline the webbing. Use Burnt Umber in a thin enough layer to flow well off the brush, but not so thin that it runs, creating a mess. This is delicate work, so err on the side of getting paint on the webbing, as you can go back and touch that up later.

Apply the same Burnt Umber to the seams where the coat sleeves meet the coat. Adding a shadow here, and later a highlight, will help simulate a sewn seam.

Highlights are applied using the base mixture with more Khaki added. Apply it to all the areas that would receive some light, such as tops of folds. Apply four to five very thin layers, as this will help keep the color transitions looking smooth.

Follow the main highlights with a lighter mix for the extreme or higher highlights. You can do this by adding just Khaki to these areas, and to lighten that, gradually add Vallejo British Tank Crew Highlights (No. 70.321).

After the trousers base coat (see p. 54), add more German Camo Black Brown, almost pure, to create a seam down each leg. I did this now so I could apply highlights and shadows to the adjoining areas and try to simulate different cuts of cloth. Any slipups can easily be corrected later.

Use the same seam mixture underneath the jacket where it meets the top of the trousers and on the trousers' fly seam.

Next, add shadows on the larger folds applying thin layers of the base mixed with German Camo Black Brown. Again, thin layers are vital so as not to leave noticeable brushstrokes.

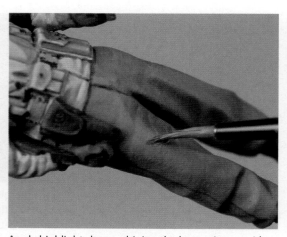

Add more German Camo Black Brown to the initial shadow mix to use on darker shadow areas, such as underneath a pant leg fold.

Apply highlights by combining the base mixture with more Muddy Brown, then thin layers of just Muddy Brown, and lastly a mix of Muddy Brown + Vallejo Flat Earth (No. 70.983).

The final highlight can be almost pure Flat Earth. Apply it to the highest areas, top of sharp folds and outside of the seams running down the legs.

Both figures are now completely painted. I only added a few Archer decals to the helmets, armbands, and shoulders to finish each figure.

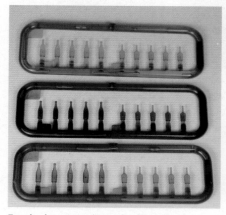

For the loot I used MiniArt Miniatures Champagne & Cognac Bottles with Crates (No. 35575) and Beer Bottles & Wooden Crates (No. 35574), which I airbrushed with Tamiya Smoke (X-19), then Krylon Matte, before painting on labels and finishing the glass with Pledge Floor Gloss (PFG).

There also was a fix to the Jeep's decals. Here you see the white and yellow Chrysler symbol in the middle of the words Military Police on the windshield frame's bottom. I did research, plus knew from my own MP experience that this should be white and blue. The company agreed it was a mistake, so I carefully repainted it white and blue.

In this and the two photos atop the next page you can see the extra details of the items the MPs have with them: beer, cognac, champagne, and a magazine. The driver seems to have already started tasting the spoils, as he has one bottle open in his left hand.

7.4 Tanker in Winter Overalls and Field Jacket

When I first saw the 1/35 scale Tamiya US Tank Crew (European Theater) set (No. 35347), I simply had to buy it and build a few of the figures. These fit well into a Sherman tank vignette or diorama, but a few are great stand-alone figures.

First, I wanted to build the tanker standing in winter overalls and a winter combat hood.

The overalls (actual nomenclature Trousers, Combat, Winter) were made of an 8.2-oz. cotton shell with the same wool blanket lining as the Combat Field Jacket or Tanker Jacket. There were two patterns. The one here was the second pattern and consisted of hardware in front with suspender adjustment clips, a front zipper, and short zippers at the ankles.

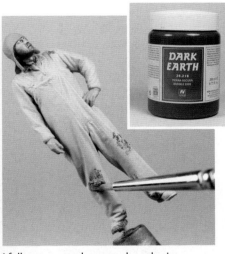

I follow my usual approach and prime the figure, then paint the face. I also base coated the tanker's hood. I wanted to show weathering on the figure, so prior to undercoating him I took an old paint brush and applied Vallejo Dark Earth (No. 26.218) to the knees, bottom of the trousers, and parts of the boots.

Here's what I used to base coat the tanker's clothing.

COLORS:
Hood: War Front from Scale 75 Pale Earth (No. SW-34) + Vallejo Burnt Umber (No. 70.941)
Field Jacket: Vallejo German Camo Beige (No. 70.821) + Vallejo Burnt Umber
Overalls: Vallejo US Field Drab (No. 70.873) + Vallejo Burnt Umber

FIELD JACKET

Once the base coat is dry, I add shadows by gradually adding more Burnt Umber into the base mix on the jacket beneath the overalls.

Then add almost straight Burnt Umber to the deep areas and to outline the overalls, pockets, and zipper.

Deeper areas are painted pure Burnt Umber and in a few of the darkest areas I add a tad of Scale 75 Flat Black (No. SC-00) to the Burnt Umber.

Shadows and outlining are complete, but the clothing appears too stark. However, the colors will be blended during the highlight stage.

Highlights are applied using the base coat, plus more German Camo Beige until it's just the Camo Beige being used for the final highlight. This takes about four layers to properly highlight the figure.

Much of the outlining blends and smooths in appearance as the highlights are applied. Here I have added a few faux seams to the shoulder areas using the outline color mix.

To remedy the lack of detail on the collar I used Field Drab and German Camo Beige, then added more Camo Beige to simulate texture. Later I applied dark lines using Black and Burnt Umber.

OVERALLS

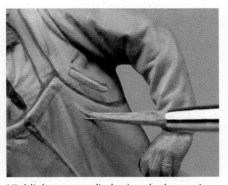

Shadows on the overalls are created by adding more Burnt Umber to the Field Drab mix. In the deeper areas even more Burnt Uber is applied. I also use the mix to run a seam down the front of the overalls to simulate where a zipper would be.

Highlights are applied using the base mix with German Camo Beige added. I like to add surrounding colors to help unify the colors in all the clothing. This doesn't work with all colors, but works well with these.

To make the figure pop I add bright edging to the overalls and jacket. I used the last highlight color for the jacket and overalls, then added AK Interactive Decomposed Flesh (No. AK11058). Here I turn my brush sideways and drag it along the edges.

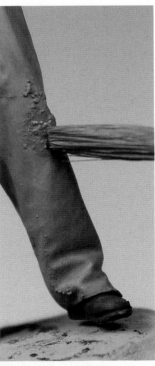

The last step entails adding the same highlight mix as a seam down the overalls front where the zipper would be. This helps simulate a folded piece of material hiding the zipper.

All the highlights and shadows have been applied, but I also added some fake seams to the hood, using the same process as for the overalls. This provides extra detail and makes your figure stand apart from others. You can also see that I added some extra bright small, simulated folds to the front top of the overalls.

The jacket and overalls are complete after they both receive details such as zippers and overall hardware. The deepest folds also get a deep shadow of black to help add definition. If you look closely you can even see that a small detail was painted onto his hand, a wedding band. The manufacturer sculpted in this nice little touch, so don't ignore it.

Weathering the overalls was next. I took a thin wash of the base mixture plus Burnt Umber and began dabbing it onto the knees. Dabbing helps make the patterns random. I like to make weathering or stains appear as if they are ground into the fabric, not just painted on. I have found the best way to do this is by adding more base mix, then gradually darkening it.

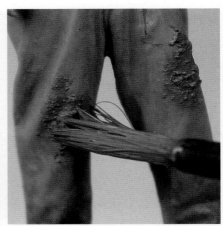

I also applied the mix a little more heavily to the lower legs and boots.

Here a darker mix of Burnt Umber and Flat Black is applied in very thin layers. You can see that random blotches have been applied, as well.

This final mixture also can be dabbed across the muddy knees to simulate the irregularities of dirt and mud.

For the finishing touches of weathering, I used AK's Terrains Muddy Ground (No. AK8017) for ground cover and on the bottom of boots. This helps the figure blend with the base and appear more natural.

DECALS

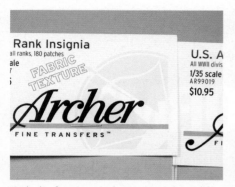

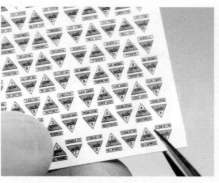

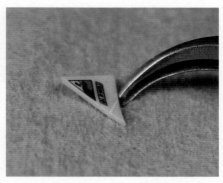

With the figure complete I wanted to add a unit patch and rank to the jacket's sleeves. The kit provided decals, but I had two sets from Archer Fine Transfers that I feel are superior and easier to use. These also do not have a decal film, which makes them appear more realistic.

I used the 2nd Armored Division Hell on Wheels from Archer. Decal scissors from Tamiya are best for cutting out decals.

Set the decal in water for about 25 to 30 seconds, then remove it with tweezers and place it on a paper towel to absorb excess water.

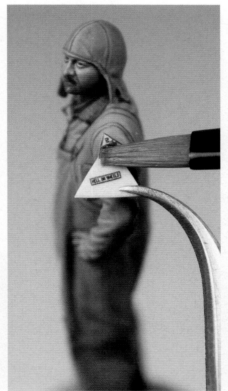

Use a soft brush and add a little water to the area where the decal will be applied.

The decal is then placed on the shoulder with the damp brush and adjusted until correctly positioned.

Finally, use a cotton swab to press the decal into place. I use a hair dryer to set it. Once all the decals are applied, I brush Vallejo Matt Medium (No. 70.540) over them, and the figure is complete.

GERMAN UNIFORMS

Mastering Field Gray, Panzer Black, and camouflage

KEVIN THOMPSON PHOTO

The idea for my "Propaganda" diorama came after I saw Tamiya's 1/35 scale German Infantry Set
(Mid War) (No. TAM35371). I had previously seen the Bravo 6 figures of an officer and a soldier
taking pictures. They were Herr Officer (No. B6-35133) and Kriegsberichter (No. B6-35125).
They simply seemed like a great fit for the scene I wanted to create.

8.1 Soldiers Diorama (various shades of Field Gray)

I was not sure how to pose the figures for my "Propaganda" diorama to deliver the propaganda message, but that's when I found Great North Roads Dioramas, Vignettes and Accessories for the Discerning Military Modeler. Quite a mouthful, but this company had the building I needed.

I wanted to show German soldiers, an NCO, an officer, and a cameraman posing for a photo opportunity that said everything was going great in the war, hence the "Propaganda" title. The scene needed to look staged, but I purposely did not want a lot of rubble or debris, although naturally there would be some. I also wanted to make a prop door to replace what naturally would have been destroyed. I also wanted to convey that after the soldiers did as they were instructed, they would be rewarded with beer, magazines, and newspapers.

During construction I was going to need to do a lot of field gray uniform painting, along with helmets, etc. There also would be extra details needed to create the proper atmosphere, and of course a building.

Because there would be so much field gray, I decided to just show the process of painting one shade, but list other mixes that I used and that you can try. I used various field gray mixes on each of the soldiers, except for three. These three would just have some different amount of the basic paints mixed, thus creating slightly different shades.

Here is a list of the different mixes that I used. The highlights were usually a lighter version of the base coat's lightest color, created by adding Vallejo Sunny Skintone (No. 70.845) to the mixture.

FIELD GRAY
BASE COAT MIXES

1. Kneeling Soldier: Andrea No. 1 Base + No. 5 First Shadow from the Andrea Field Gray Set (No. ACS-010)

2. Soldier with Rifle standing at door: AK Interactive German Field Gray (No. AK 11154) + Vallejo Yellow Olive (No. 70.892)

3. Soldier with Machine Gun: AK Interactive German Field Gray + Vallejo Yellow Olive

4. Cigarette-smoking soldier: AK Interactive German Field Gray + AK Interactive Command Green (No. AK11155)

5. Soldier taking pictures: Vallejo Field Gray (No. 70.830 + No. 5 First Shadow from Andrea Field Gray Set

6. Officer: Scale 75 Field Gray (No. SC-46) + Scale 75 War Front Field Gray No. 1 (No. SW-38)

7. Soldier holding ammo can: AK Interactive German Field Gray + Scale 75 Field Gray

 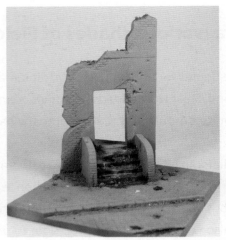 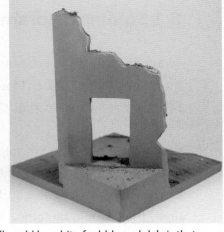

The diorama centers around the building and steps, which are ceramic and extremely cleanly cast, so they need minimal clean-up. A few parts were glued together using wood glue. I wanted to add extra textures, so I used Vallejo Earth Textures Dark Earth (No. 26.218) applied to various locations with an old, damp paintbrush.

I wanted the area clean, but thought there still could be a bit of rubble and debris that might have fallen from the building. I used some old Verlinden red bricks that I had in my spares box, but first I placed them in a plastic bag and crushed them with a hammer. I then applied diluted wood glue to spots where I wanted rubble before placing the broken pieces. Once I had them in position, I used an eye dropper to apply drops of diluted wood glue over the rubble.

 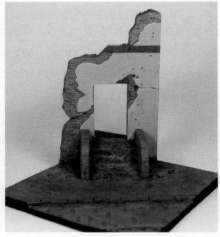 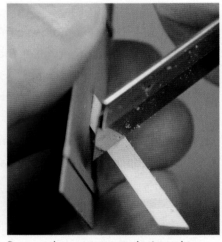

The scene has been painted with various shades of red, browns, and orange from AK Interactive, Vallejo, and Scale 75 for the bricks, and gray shades for the sidewalk.

I finished the base using a variety of acrylic washes from Vallejo along with pastels from AK Interactive.

Because the scene was to depict a photo op, I wanted a staged door as a backdrop to fill the empty doorway. I used a spare wooden door from an older kit, but didn't want it to look new, as the original door likely would have been destroyed when the building was damaged. I did not have the framework for a doorway, so thought it fitting that the door would be propped up by another piece of wood. I cut and glued a piece of sheet styrene behind the door. Once set, I used a hobby saw blade to gouge wood grain into the plastic.

Using a Scotch Brite pad, I removed the debris from the saw blade on the new wood support.

Using styrene half round, I made a decorative design on the door and used a scrap piece of styrene and a piece of copper wire to simulate a door handle.

Turning to the figures, I undercoated the machine gun soldier and painted his flesh and accessories before applying highlights and shadows to his uniform.

I started by applying medium shadows to all shadow areas, including around the pockets, the pocket flaps, and along the web belt, always using very controlled layers. My highlight mix is the base coat of AK German Field Gray with a little more Vallejo Yellow Olive added.

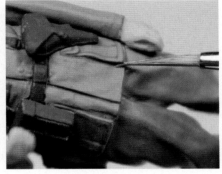

Darker shadows are applied where the pockets meet the coat, under the collar, the seam where the coat front buttons, and on pocket flaps. For this use Vallejo Yellow Olive mixed with a small amount of Scale 75 Flat Black (No. SC-00).

Next, outline the pockets, seams on the pockets, and seams at the coat's bottom with a mix of Vallejo Yellow Olive and Vallejo German Cam Black Brown. Apply with a brush that holds a good point and with properly thinned paint to avoid globs.

Here the shadows and outlining are complete, but I still need to add them to the bottom of the coat's front.

Highlight application is next. I work in sections, here working on the lower front. Highlights consist of the base with a bit more AK German Field Gray. I continue building up layers until I'm just using pure Field Gray. Lastly I add a small amount of Vallejo Sunny Skintone to the Field Gray.

Highlights finished, I add just a small amount more of Vallejo Sunny Skintone to the Field Gray and edge the pockets, seam lines, and cuffs. This, next to the earlier darker outlining, helps the fabric stand out and helps separate fabric areas.

TROUSERS

Next, work on the trousers. Unlike the tunics, I wanted to keep the trousers close in color on all the figures except for the officer and cameraman. I thought that these would be the two soldiers who would have more of an office type job, whereas the other soldiers' uniforms would show more wear.

The base colors for the officer's trousers are Scale 75 Field Gray (No. SC-46) + War Front Field Gray No.1 (No. SW-38), while the cameraman's trousers are Vallejo Field Gray + Andrea No. 5 First Shadow from Andrea's Field Gray set.

The remaining soldiers' trousers were a basecoat of Vallejo Field Gray + Vallejo Bronze Green (No. 70.897).

Adding shadows begins with a mix of the base plus more Bronze Green. This should be thin because, in this example, there is a long shadow area and if not well thinned, the paint will likely leave a big brush mark. If you are not comfortable with just adding water to paint these larger areas, you can use the "Secret Sauce" (1 drop of Vallejo Retarder (No. 70.597) and 15 drops of water) or Vallejo Glaze Medium (No. 70.596).

Next, gradually darken the shadow mix by adding more Bronze Green to the mixture. Apply the new mix to the deeper folds. It is best to apply this with a sharply pointed brush so that you can have better control. Use this color sparingly and only for the deepest shadows.

Initial highlights are applied to all the high areas and the tops of folds using the base mixture with more Vallejo German Field Gray added. Because these colors are fairly dark, it's important to keep them thin to avoid brushstrokes. Sometimes you must do a long, large fold, so remember to use a brush large enough to get this process done, again applying thin, controlled layers.

I then move on to the higher highlights, those areas receiving more light. For this I use German Field Gray by itself, then gradually add a small amount of Vallejo Sunny Skintone.

Follow that with a lighter tone for the highest, brightest highlights. I add a small amount of Sunny Skintone to the highlight mix in the last step, applying it sparingly to the highest areas. Now the trousers are finished.

EXTRA, BUT NEEDED, DETAILS

A few things came up, as they nearly always do, during assembly and painting that require thinking outside the box. One of the main concerns was how to add weapons and slings to painted figures and not cause any damage.

The NCO needed his weapon glued into his hand prior to painting the figure. This caused a bit of a problem with trying to get the gun's sling attached with correct folds. I used an ABER photo-etch part, then carefully painted it.

This figure was challenging, but became one of my favorites in this group. While the rifle fit in his hands during dry-fitting, after primer and paint were added, it would not. After carefully carving away some paint I was able to squeeze the rifle into place, but I needed no glue for it to remain in his hands! I then added the sling, knowing I'd have to carefully paint the weapon, then the sling, being careful to not cause myself any extra work ...

... so I carefully painted the rifle. This step shows that with patience and a hair dryer, you can use acrylic paint directly on plastic parts. Primer is not always necessary, especially for small items.

COMPLETED DIORAMA DETAILS

8.2 Panzer Black

PAINTING BLACK

This figure wears a black panzer jacket, sometimes referred to as a Wrap over or Wrapper because it featured a double-breasted front. The jacket was made from black wool and was short-waisted with no additional pockets. It also contained four large plastic buttons at the bottom to secure the jacket. Three smaller buttons toward the jacket's top were used if the soldier wanted to fasten the top in cold weather.

There were two types of panzer jackets, one for the Heer (Army), the other for the Waffen SS. These were similar, but had a few differences.

The Heer collar tips were more pointed and the Waffen's more rounded. The Heer version also had a seam running down the middle of the back because it was made in two sections, while the Waffen version was made from a single piece of cloth.

I prime the figure as usual, airbrushing with Tamiya Sky Gray (No. XF-19). I prefer this because I feel the paint has a good bite and is less likely to rub off during handling.

Next, apply the base coat using a mix of Andrea Black Paint set No. 6 and No. 4. This base is a very dark gray and will serve as the middle shadows, allowing me to use pure black later for deeper shadows. Apply the base in several thin layers, drying between each with a hair dryer.

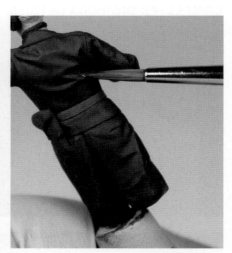

To create the first set of highlights, apply more of the Black No. 4 into the base coat mix. Build this up gradually to avoid a harsh looking line, again keeping the layers thin.

Higher highlights get tricky because you'll need to add more No. 4 to the base mix and apply it to small areas. But because it's black you'll not want to use it on many high areas, as it can look streaky. Be careful!

If your highlights look too bright, you can blend them and reduce this by adding glazes to the areas with the base coat mixture. At this point you also can add pure Black No. 6 in deep shadows or a flat black.

The final step is edging. Use a good, pointed brush and be careful. Take your time. In areas with the highest color highlight I use the side of the brush. This helps separate certain areas and give the coat life so it doesn't look flat.

The jacket is complete, but I wanted to try out the kit decals for badges and insignias. After they were applied I used my hair dryer to set them, then airbrushed Vallejo Matt Medium (No. 70.540) over the figure.

Next, I added microphone wiring to the figure using .10 lead wire that I bought at my local fly-fishing shop. Before attaching the wires, I took a small section of sheet lead and wrapped it around the throat microphone wires, creating a switch box. The wires were attached with super glue.

The final step is carefully painting the wiring using a mix of Vallejo Burnt Red (No. 70.814) + Scale 75 Blood Red (No. SC-36).

ITALIAN CAMOUFLAGE TROUSERS

HEER PANZER OFFICER

Around 1943, following the disarmament of most of Italy's armed forces, the Germans had stocks of Italian material that they used to help meet their increase in demand for equipment.

Here I'll show how I replicate the Italian Camo using the AK German Uniform Italian Pattern paint set (No. AK11681).

Begin by giving the trousers a base coat of AK Command Green (No. AK11155) + AK Gunship Green (No. AK11150). I also made a darker mix of Command Green + Scale 75 Flat Black (No. SC-00) and placed a seam down the outside of each leg.

I then add the brown islands to the trousers using AK Hull Red (No. AK11108). Apply these with a No. 0 brush using irregular patterns.

Brown islands complete, apply ochre islands, again applied randomly, but next to a few browns. Use AK Light Earth (No. AK1115). Painting a "yellow" color is challenging, as it requires several thin applications for good coverage, yet without leaving paint strokes.

After rechecking references for pattern accuracy, the camo is ready.

Next, add highlights to the initial colors as previously demonstrated in this, and other, chapters. Again, keep the mixtures extremely thin.

HIGHLIGHT MIXTURES ARE:
Base Green: AK Gunship Green + AK Faded Green (No. AK11135)
Brown Islands: AK Hull Red + AK Deep Brown (No. AK11102)
Ochre Islands: AK Middle Stone + AK Light Earth (No. AK1115)

The result is this realistic German officer figure that fits into a vignette or into a diorama that you design.

RUSSIAN UNIFORMS

Mastering Gymnastyorka uniforms, shadowing, and re-creating a flag

KEVIN THOMPSON PHOTO

I only had to see the 1/35 scale kit, The Flag over Berlin (No. SW35-049), to know I'd love painting it. Scale 75's kit depicts the famous Yevgeny Khaldei photo from March 2, 1945. Over the years it has come to represent the Soviets' victory over Nazi Germany. The kit also would allow me to demonstrate how to paint several Russian uniforms and create a realistic flag for the scene.

There are many elements here. First, the site is on top of the Reichstag building, important because it was considered magnificent and recognizable. Second, Khaldei had the Soviet flag used in the photo with him. It was made from table-cloths.

Soldiers in the scene are wearing the Gymnastyorka uniforms of the times. The one planting the flag is wearing the pre-1943 version, which had a collar, while the sergeant and one standing at the bottom are wearing the post-1943 tunics.

9.1 Tunic, Trousers, and Creating a Flag

The diorama's base is beautifully cast in resin, and once assembled with super glue, is quickly ready for primer. I also assembled and placed the figures on the base to assure a proper fit.

After checking the fit I knew that I'd need to glue the top soldier on the structure before painting, plus fill any seams with putty. This would require finishing the stonework before painting the figure. I also now added Vallejo Earth Textures to the base.

The flag that is supplied in the kit is just a piece of paper with the flag printed on it. I wanted something better, so I used dry transfers of Soviet flags from Archer Fine Transfers (No. AR35018).

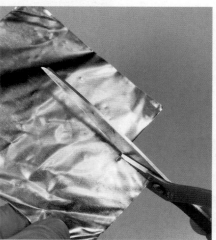

I traced the size I'd need for the flag on a piece of thin tin and then cut it to size with scissors. Once complete, I simply transferred the flag to the tin and bent it to shape.

SERGEANT'S TUNIC

I began by base coating the sergeant's tunic with a mix of AK Russian Green (No. 11430) + Vallejo German Camo Black Brown (No. 70.822). I kept this mix slightly on the darker side so that I could add highlights that were not too stark, yet still noticeable.

After applying several thin coats of paint the tunic is complete and I decided to paint on the sergeant's rank. Doing it now would make it easier to correct any mistakes.

The front of the sergeant's body will be pressed against the pillar, so it will be in shadow. I darkened the base mixture by adding more German Camo Black Brown and applied it to his front almost like a controlled wash. It needed to be substantially darker than other areas.

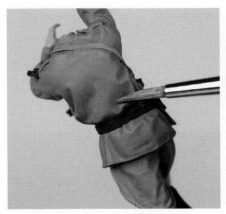

For the back's shadows I apply the same mix of the base and German Camo Black Brown, just not as much as on the front.

Adding more German Camo Black Brown to the mix, I create deeper shadows along the cuffs ...

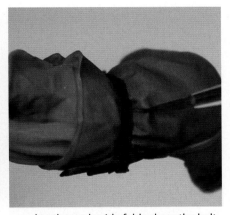

... and to the underside folds along the belt where the tunic has been tucked in.

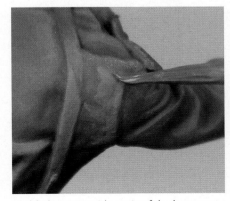

Highlights start with a mix of the base coat + AK Interactive Canvas Tone (No. AK11436) applied to the top of all folds and the shoulders. It looks stark now, but I will blend the highlights next.

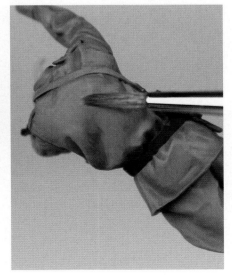

I blend the highlights and shadows with the base coat using "Special Sauce," something I learned from Don Suratos, a talented artist. This blends the colors' edges to create a uniform look.

SPECIAL SAUCE: Mix 1 part Vallejo Retarder Medium (No. 70.597) with 15 parts water. I dip my paintbrush in the Special Sauce, then into the paint. This makes the paint flow easier and not dry as quickly so it blends with surrounding colors.

STANDING SOLDIER & FLAG SOLDIER

The standing soldier and the soldier attaching the flag are painted with the same colors with slight variations of base mixes. This keeps them looking similar, but not like their uniforms are from the same cloth, and also shows different wear and tear.

The standing soldier's tunic and all base coat colors are applied to his cap and pants. So he is now ready for highlights and shadows to be applied.

BASE COAT COLORS:
Tunic and Cap: AK Canvas Tone (No. AK11436) + Vallejo Burnt Umber (No. 70.941)
Pants: Vallejo English Uniform (No. 70.921) + Vallejo German Camo Black Brown (No. 70.822) Ratio is EU 90% + GCBB 10%

Shadows are applied to all the main folds using the base mix with more German Camo Black Brown added.

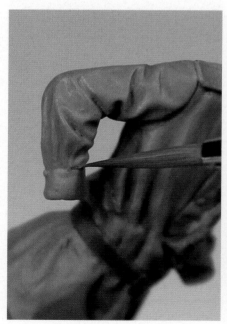

Next, apply a dark shadow to seams, cuffs, deep folds, and along the belt and strap. This should be a darker version of the previous shadow mix—not pure German Camo Black Brown, but very close.

With shadows complete on the tunic, begin applying highlights, a mix of the base and Canvas Tone.

Add several highlight layers, gradually adding more Canvas Tone until you are applying just pure Canvas Tone. Always apply the lighter highlights to areas receiving more light, such as the top of the shoulders, and top of the forearms.

The highest highlights are applied with a mixture of AK Canvas Tone plus Panzer Aces 321 Highlight British Tanker. Apply thin layers to the edges of the cuffs and collar.

The tunic is now complete with all highlights and shadows added.

Next, apply shadows to the pants using the base coat mixed with a little German Camo Black Brown.

A darker mixture of the previous shadow color is then applied to the underside of folds and deep recess areas. This is almost pure German Camo Black Brown.

Highlights are applied to the top of folds with a mixture of the base and Panzer Aces Highlight British Tanker. These are applied in thin layers. Again, gradually build these layers to avoid brushstrokes.

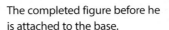

Finally, apply the highest highlights to the most prominent areas by adding more of the Panzer Aces Highlight British Tanker in thin layers.

The completed figure before he is attached to the base.

PAINTING SMALLER SCALE

Brighter highlights, darker shadows work best to create realism

Smaller scale figures have become more popular, especially among modelers who enjoy using figures in their aircraft and armor dioramas. The 1/48 scale figures are particularly popular for this, and more new kits are being produced in that scale. Another plus for 1/48 scale, or smaller figures, is that they take up less space to display.

10.1 A 1/48 Figure

But you'll soon realize when painting smaller scale figures that you can't paint them exactly as you would larger ones. If you do, they will seem flat and not have the pop that you are familiar with on larger figures.

You can combat this by painting more vibrant or brighter highlights next to a darker shadow color than you would with larger scale figures.

Trust me, it will seem like too much at first. But realize that the average viewer will be looking at these from a distance of 2 to 3 feet. If you don't make the highlights and shadows a little more exaggerated, the viewer will not notice all the figure's details.

Here's an example of how I paint a smaller scale figure.

BASE COAT

First prime and add a base coat to the small scale soldier, applying the base to the entire figure before adding highlights, shadows or details. This helps me identify what colors I want to go with for each portion of the figure.

Here the flesh is base coated using Citadel Acrylics Cadian Fleshtone + Citadel's Bugman's Glow. Keep this on the darker side, then add additional shadows under the chin, eye sockets, and around the nose by using Vallejo Dark Red (No. 70.946).

The hands receive the same base coat as the face, and Vallejo Dark Red is applied between each finger to create separation.

The eyes (yes, they need attention even in this scale), are first painted Vallejo Burnt Umber (No. 70.941). Then I place a tiny dot of Vallejo Basic Skintone (No. 70.815) on the right side of the eyes to give the appearance that they are looking to his left.

Here you see the completed eyes. Painting eyes in this scale requires a brush with a sharp point.

Next, add highlights at the cheekbone, chin, nose tip and upper lip. Use the base mix with more Cadian Fleshtone and applied in layers. Pure Fleshtone is then added, mixed with a bit of Vallejo Beige Red (No. 70.804) and lastly pure Beige Red.

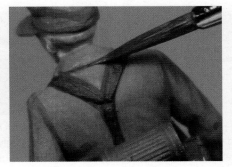

The jacket's base coat is from Andrea's Field Gray paint set, a mix of No. 1 + No. 5. The shadows and outlining of all the areas are the base mix with more No. 5 added. My goal was to make this rather stark so all the other areas would stand out.

Here you see the figure with all outlining and shadows completed.

For the coat I add highlights using the base mix and more Field Gray No. 1. Final highlights are the No. 1 + Vallejo Basic Skintone (No. 70.815). Here you also see the trousers after given a base coat of AK Interactive Command Green (No. AK 11155) mixed with Field Gray No. 5. Highlights are achieved by adding more Command Green to the base, while shadows were created by adding more No. 5 to the base, then pure No. 5 in the deepest areas.

I also add a false seam to both the inside and outside of each leg. I use No. 5 Field Gray for the dark line and a mix of Command Green + Vallejo Basic Skintone.

The boot's upper section is painted with a base of Vallejo Khaki (No. 70.988) + Scale 75 War Front Pale Earth (No. SW-34). I kept this on the dark side and added more Khaki + Basic Skintone for the highlights and then more Pale Earth to create shadows.

I painted the ammo pouches with a mixture of Scale 75 War Front Camo Ocher Brown (No. SW-12) + Scale 75 War Front Pale Earth. A wash of Vallejo Burnt Umber (No. 70.941) is then applied to all areas of the ammo pouches.

Adding highlights is next using the base along with more Camo Ocher Brown and finally applying Vallejo Khaki (No. 70.988) on the highest highlights.

The figure is complete and is positioned with the one brush, a No. 0, that I used to paint everything on the figure. I stress again that a good paintbrush with a strong point is the key tool to help you improve your painting.

Here's the completed figure next to a U.S. dime, giving perspective as to the figure's size.

This side view of the completed figure shows his weapon and the figure's base.

PAINTING BUSTS

Larger surface areas allow for finer detailing, blending of skin tones

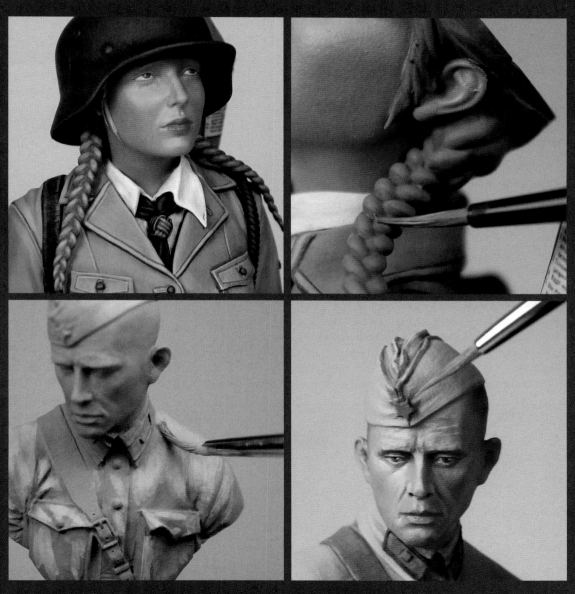

Busts are bigger and provide much larger surface areas for painting. That means they require finer detail work and care with thin layers so that brush strokes are not evident. Remember, a bust will be seen much more closely than small scale figures in a diorama.

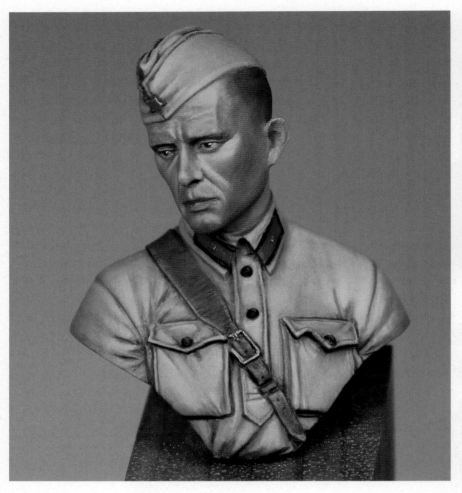

First, clean the bust and airbrush it with Tamiya Sky Gray (No. X-19) as a primer.

11.1 Red Army Lieutenant 1941

During WWII the Soviet Army's lower ranking officers were issued M32/M35 Gymnasterka tunics. These shirts were made of cotton and featured three buttons down the front and one on each breast pocket. The collar had tabs which told the rank and type of unit the soldier was assigned to.

Here I paint FER Miniatures' 1/16 scale Red Army Lieutenant starting with my airbrush.

I then add a base coat of Scale 75 War Front Russian Uniform (No. SW-45) + Vallejo Panzer Aces Highlight British Tanker 321, applied with an airbrush.

NOTE I originally planned to hand-brush this and had laid down a flesh base coat, but then decided to use the airbrush, which helps blend the colors. Thus the face has a flesh look.

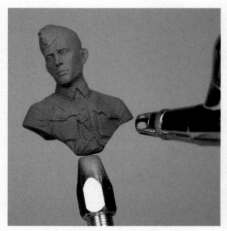

Airbrushing up from the bottom with a darker mixture of the base with more Russian Uniform added creates a deeper shadowy area.

Here you can see the bust with the initial darker shade complete.

Now a lighter mixture of the base coat, which includes more Panzer Aces Highlight British Tanker, is airbrushed from above to create initial highlights.

This step is different from my normal procedure. I wanted to sketch out the bright highlights that would be visible, so I added pure Panzer Aces Highlight British Tanker to all the areas that would receive a highlight.

The bust after I completed the sketching. At this stage I asked myself, what have I done? It will all come together, at least that is what I told myself!

I then airbrushed the base coat color in a light mist over the whole bust to blend the colors. This must not be a heavy application, because you still want to see the highlights and shadows.

The first thin highlight layers to be added consists of Panzer Aces Highlight British Tanker + Scale 75 War Front Braun (No. SW-028).

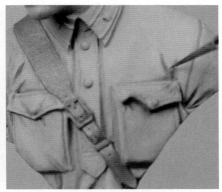

The shadows then receive gradual layers of Russian Uniform. The darkest shadows are a mix of Russian Uniform + Vallejo Burnt Umber (No. 70.941).

Thin applications of Russian Uniform are then used to outline different areas.

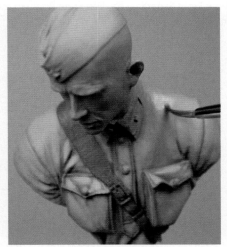

More intense highlights are added in thin layers using a mix of Scale 75 War Front Braun + Scale 75 War Front Sahara Sand (No. SW-36).

I finish the tunic by edging it with War Front Sahara Sand + Vallejo Green Gray (No. 70.971).

THE PILOTKA HAT

The lieutenant is wearing a Pilotka, or garrison hat. The name Pilotka is derived from the word "pilot," as these hats were part of the Russian Air Force pilots' uniform in WWI. They became a staple and were used even as late as the 1980s.

A base coat of War Front Russian Uniform + Panzer Aces Highlight British Tanker had previously been applied during the tunic painting. Here I add more Russian Uniform paint to the mix for the shadows.

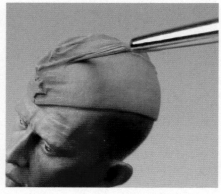

I apply the same mixture along the hat's seam lines.

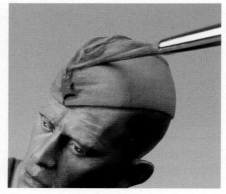

The same shadow and seam areas are then given a darker application by adding Vallejo Burnt Umber and Russian Uniform to the base mix.

Highlights are then applied using the base coat + more Panzer Aces Highlight British Tanker.

Additional highlights are applied by adding War Front Braun and War Front Sahara Sand to the mix.

Highlights become more concentrated after adding more War Front Braun to the mix.

Extreme highlights and edges are almost pure War Front Braun.

Here you see the completed bust with all its subtle shades of brown melded together for a realistic look.

11.2 League of German Girls, Berlin 1945

During the war there were many types of organizations in Germany but one that is not readily modeled is the BDM, Bund Deutscher Mädel, or League of German Girls. During this time, it was the only legal youth organization for females in the Nazi party. When first introduced it was comprised of two age groups/sections, the first for ages 10 to 14 called Jungmädelbund, the Young Girls' League, and second for ages 14 to 18. But in 1938 another section was added, the BDM-Werk Glaube und Schönheit, or Faith and Beauty Society, for young women ages 17 to 21. After the Nazi surrender in 1945, the organization ceased to exist and was outlawed in October of that year by the Allied Control Council.

When I saw this wonderfully sculpted bust of a Bund Deutscher Mädel from Kilgore HD Miniatures I decided it would make a great subject. The kit is a 1/10 scale resin kit with six beautifully cast parts. I received an early production kit that did not have the decals for the panzerfäust at the time. It does now. For my model, though, friend Chad Weyenberg made me some decals.

FLESH

Begin by priming the bust with Tamiya Sky Gray (No. XF-19) via airbrush. Because this is a young girl figure, I approached the flesh a little differently than my normal base coat. I add Scale 75 Pale Skin (No. SC-17) to the mix and airbrush it onto the highlight areas, cheekbones, forehead, tip of nose and chin.

I then begin laying in the shadows. You can do this with a brush, but since I was using my airbrush, I added Scale 75 Orcish Dermis (No. SFG-19) to all shadow areas, under the cheeks, under the chin, eyes, and alongside the nose.

I follow that by airbrushing a light covering of Scale 75 Resurrection Flesh (No. SFG-14) over the face and neck, but keep it light enough for the shadow and highlights to show through.

Next, I mix Scale 75 Light Skin (No. SC-18) with a small amount of the Resurrection Flesh to apply to the highlight areas. It is important that these applications be very thin glazes that you build up with repeated applications. Thin layers will help prevent unwanted paint strokes.

Put a little color in the cheeks by adding thin glazes of Vallejo Transparent Red (No. 70.934). Thin is the key word!

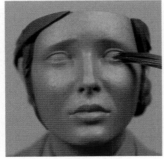

I also add a thin layer of Transparent Red to the eye sockets. This will help later when painting the eyes.

The next two steps involve applying pastels. These soft pastel colors are not overpowering, which makes them work well here.

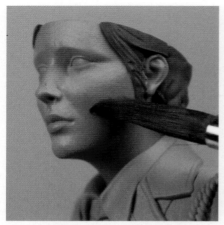

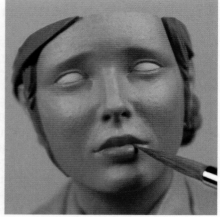

First, scrape the red pastel with a hobby knife into a small pile, then using a clean, soft brush, apply the red pastel into the figure's cheek hollows.

Do the same with a flesh- or peach-colored pastel and apply it to the cheekbones, nose, and chin.

To complete the face, paint the lips with a mixture of Scale 75 Baal Crimson (No. SF-G04) + Scale 75 Bosh Chestnut (No. SFG-35).

TUNIC

The original BDM jackets were either a blue velvet or tan. I chose the tan version, creating a base by mixing AK Interactive Ochre Khaki (No. AK11422) + Vallejo Burnt Umber (No. 70.941). Apply several thin layers and speed drying with a hair dryer.

I then add a bit more Burnt Umber to the base before applying it to the shadow areas. Deeper shadows were created by adding additional Burnt Umber to the mix.

Begin adding highlights by mixing more Ochre Khaki to the base coat mix. Apply to all the highlight areas, such as buttons, in thin and controlled glazes.

Higher highlights are achieved by adding Vallejo Panzer Aces British Tanker Highlight to the Ochre Khaki. These highlights are gradually lightened by adding more British Tanker Highlights to the mix, which is used on areas that would receive the most light.

Finally the highest highlights are created with a mixture of British Tanker Highlights + Vallejo Dark Sand (No. 70.847). This is only added to the extremely bright areas, and again is applied in thin glazes. This step will add some pop to the coat.

To add extra detail you'll want to paint edging and lining. Here you see the difference. The right side has been lined and edged vs. the left where there is only highlighting and shadowing. The right side pops, while the left side looks flat.

Here a very dark shadow color from our base is applied around the pocket to simulate seams. Use this process on the pockets, buttonholes and seams. Once completed, I went back and added the last highlight color to areas alongside the dark lining.

Finally, the jacket's lining and edging is complete. You can see that the extra effort brings the jacket to life, avoiding a flat appearance.

THE HELMET

I prime the helmet as usual, then airbrush it with AK Chocolate Brown (No. AK11113), as I want to give this a dark base before the next steps. Once it dried I sprayed the helmet with Krylon Matte Finish (No. 1311) to seal the paint.

Next, I add the main helmet color, AK German Field Gray (No. AK 11154). I apply this by tearing a sponge and dabbing it into the paint, removing the excess on a paper towel, then lightly dabbing this randomly onto the helmet. Applying the paint this way reveals the under color and gives the helmet a worn look.

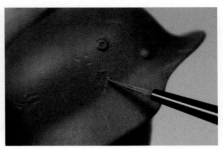

Once the base color is dry, I lighten up the base my adding a small amount of Vallejo Dark Sand (No. 70.847) using a fine-tip brush to go back and add highlights to various areas. Then I seal it with the Krylon Matte to give the helmet a nice eggshell finish.

PANZERFÄUST

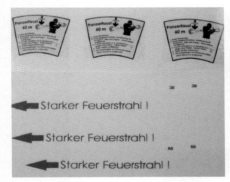

To detail the Panzerfäust as it looked in 1945, I needed accurate decals, which my friend created for me.

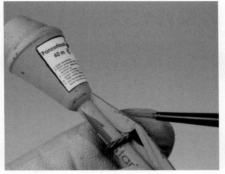

I airbrushed the Panzerfäust with Tamiya Desert Yellow (No. XF-59), then applied the decals. I used AK's Chocolate Brown to add some light chipping.

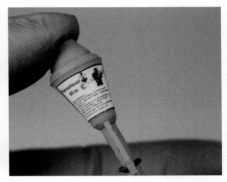

Once completed, the Panzerfäust is sprayed with Krylon Matte to seal it and give it a matte finish.

HAIR

The hair is base coated with Vallejo English Uniform (No. 70.921).

That color needs to be continually lightened with the gradual addition of Panzer Aces British Highlight 321. The last few layers are pure British Highlight with Vallejo Dark Sand (No. 70.847) added.

THE COMPLETED BUST

Assembled, the young girl figure has the look of youth, but appears equipped for war.

This is a beautiful 100mm resin figure of a WWII US Air Force Tuskegee Airman from Thunderbird Miniatures.

Warriors Miniatures cast this 120mm resin WWII Battle of the Bulge soldier wearing a US Army wool overcoat.

enjoyed creating this snowy vignette from a 1/35 scale plastic German POWs kit from MiniArt

Verlinden cast this spectacular and expressive 120mm resin figure of a WWII US Navy Pacific pilot

This 1/35 scale resin figure of a WWII US Army officer is by Alpine Miniatures. I added the snow!

Custom Dioramics created Incoming, a finely detailed 1/10 scale resin bust of a WWII US sniper.

This German officer, Wehrmacht Hauptmann Barbarossa, circa 1941, is a 120mm resin bust by FER Miniatures.

Evolution Miniatures created this 1/35 resin figure of a WWII Russian soldier, circa 1943-1945.

CONTRIBUTORS

In preparing for and writing this book I have been fortunate to have had many people in my corner who have been a tremendous help. That includes individuals and businesses, and the book would not have been possible without them.

I would like to say a special thank you to these people and their companies, while also sharing where you can contact them to buy many of the items used in painting and finishing the figures and projects in the book.

Thanks again to these individuals and their businesses!

Redgrassgames S.A
144 Rue Lecourbe 75015 Paris
www.redgrassgames.com
Vivien Massad, owner

Zem Brush Mfg.
www.zembrush.com
skevos@zembrush.com
Skevos Zembillas, owner

The Brushman
TheBrushman@hotmail.co.uk
David Jackson, owner

Royal Model
Royal Model di R. Reale
Via E. Montale 19
95030 Pedara (CT) Italy
tel.+39 095 7800707
fax:+39 095 2937848
info@royalmodel.com
www.royalmodel.com
Roberto Reale, owner

Archer Fine Transfers
(Out of business)
305 NW Railroad St.
Youngsville, NC 27596
Woody Vondracek, owner

Bravo 6 Miniatures
www.bravo6.diorama.ru
Vladimir Demchenko, owner

Scale 75 USA
351 Bank St.
Suite 101
Southlake, Texas 76092
817-329-4860
Support: info@scale75USA.com
Wholesale Orders: sales@scale75usa.com
Brian Howard

ETA Diorama
www.eta-diorama.com
Yannis Papadopoulos, owner

Mark Twain Hobby Center
2793 West Clay St.
Saint Charles, MO 63301
636-946-2816
www.hobby1.com
Kevin Thompson

MiniArt Models Ltd.
144 B Kharkivske Highway, 02091
Kiev, Ukraine
Tel/Fax: +380443371815
www.miniart-models.com
art@miniart-models.com
support@miniart-models.com

Rado Miniatures
www.radominiaturesworld.com
Radek Pituch, owner

Great North Roads
greatnorthroads.co.uk
Simon Farrugia, owner

MDMB Modelbouw
www.mdmbmodelbouw.nl
Marco Doese, owner

Tartar Miniatures
www.tartarminiatures.com
Sergey Savenkov, owner

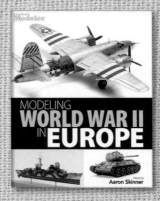
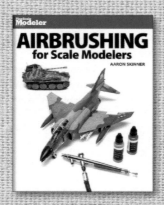
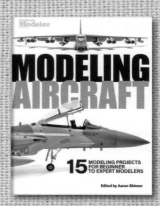